Vive le Vegan!

P9-DEE-103

Vive le Vegan!

SIMPLE, DELECTABLE RECIPES
FOR THE EVERYDAY VEGAN FAMILY

Dreena Burton

ARSENAL PULP PRESS

VANCOUVER

VIVE LE VEGAN!
Copyright © 2004 by Dreena Burton

All rights reserved. No part of this book may be reproduced or used in any form by any means – graphic, electronic or mechanical – without the prior written permission of the publisher, except by a reviewer, who may use brief excerpts in a review, or in the case of photocopying in Canada, a license from Access Copyright.

ARSENAL PULP PRESS
103 - 1014 Homer Street
Vancouver, B.C.
Canada V6B 2W9
arsenalpulp.com

The publisher gratefully acknowledges the support of the Government of Canada through the Book Publishing Industry Development Program for its publishing activities.

Interior design by Electra Design Group
Production assistance by Judy Yeung
Cover design by Solo
Cover photographs by Rosalee Hiebert
Author photograph by Judith Nicholson-Jeffries

Printed and bound in Canada

The author and publisher assert that the information contained in this book is true and complete to the best of their knowledge. All recommendations are made without guarantee on the part of the author and Arsenal Pulp Press. The author and publisher disclaim any liability in connection with the use of this information. For more information, contact the publisher.

Library and Archives Canada
Cataloguing in Publication

Burton, Dreena, 1970-
    Vive le vegan! : simple delectable recipes for the everyday vegan family / Dreena Burton.

    Includes index.
    ISBN 1-55152-169-5

1. Vegan cookery. I. Title.
TX837.B88 2004   641.5'636   C2004-902954-1

Contents

For Charlotte, whose life has blessed mine.

Acknowledgments

Paul, for your support and encouragement while writing this book, and for so thoroughly marking each page with your mighty red pen! More importantly, for your love and dedication to our family that enables me to stay at home with our daughter and also pursue my passion.

Mom, for your pride and joy in my achievements (and for making the adorable hat Charlotte is wearing on the cover!). Al and Doreen, for being so keen to try my recipes and make them yourself. Tanya, for being my best friend, and always being there to lend an ear or make me laugh. Vicki, Trish, Jen, and Brenda – a new mom could not have asked for better friends (nor a cook for better fans!). My five sisters: Debbie, Donna, Diane, Dyn'se, and Dayle; special thanks to Diane for your inspiration in coming up with the title *Vive le Vegan!*, and for the enthusiasm you and Bill always have for my work. Also to Debbie and Donna for selling *The Everyday Vegan* in your fitness clubs.

Trang Duong, for sharing your Food Introduction Schedule and for the special care and attention you have given our family.

Erin Pavlina, for your endorsement and the opportunity to contribute articles to *VegFamily.com* magazine.

Alex Chwaiewsky and Manitoba Harvest, for providing me with your excellent hemp foods products to use in my recipe testing.

Those who promoted and supported my first cookbook, including Ingrid Newkirk of PETA, Erin Pavlina and Shayla Roberts of *VegFamily*, Stewart Rose of Vegetarians of Washington, John Davis of IVU, Wanda Embar of *Vegan Peace*, Joseph Connelly and Colleen Holland of *Veg News*, Christi Wymer of *A Different Daisy*, Stacey Foley, and Stephanie Porter.

Rosalee Hiebert, for the in-house photo shoot and your kindly, enthusiastic manner working with Charlotte.

Brian, Blaine, Robert, and Trish, the team at Arsenal Pulp Press, for another opportunity to work together.

To all the folks who emailed me with your kind words and questions about *The Everyday Vegan*. I value your feedback and appreciate the time you took to write me.

Finally, very special thanks to Erik Marcus of *Vegan.com*. I am deeply grateful for your support of *The Everyday Vegan*, and for your foreword to this book. Your work encourages people to eat healthier, live more compassionately, and has inspired others to take more action to promote a vegan lifestyle. I hope to have a fraction of the impact that you have had towards this goal, and thank you for all of the work you do and the help you have given me.

Foreword

by Erik Marcus

I'm pretty sure that Edvard Munch's classic painting "The Scream" was inspired by a lifelong meat-eater contemplating a switch to a vegan diet. Even today, as the natural food industry rides a twenty-year boom with no end in sight, there's a widespread misconception that veganism requires following a rigorously disciplined and thoroughly uninteresting diet. The most common question I'm asked when somebody learns I'm a vegan is, "Well, what *do* you eat?"

With the publication of *Vive le Vegan!*, I can now answer this question without saying a word – I can just hand over this book. Here we have page after page of delicious, easy-to-prepare recipes that even committed meat-eaters will find intriguing. After getting this cookbook, I immediately lent it to a couple non-vegetarian friends. The next day, I heard nothing but raves about how delicious their food turned out.

As a vegan cookbook, *Vive le Vegan* hits the spot. None of its recipes require you to spend all day in the kitchen, nor are these recipes slapped-together affairs that anyone could have improvised. I'll be turning to this book again and again when I have guests for dinner. There are also dozens of simpler recipes included here that I can make for myself in under an hour. My favorite so far is the Cannellini Bean Yam Hummus featured on page 60; I love how this hummus tastes on bread pulled right from my bread machine.

I especially admire how *Vive le Vegan!* uses healthy, whole foods ingredients to maximum effect. Eating delicious vegan food shouldn't have to mean basing your diet on sweets, fried foods, and refined flours. This book captures the amazing flavors available in fresh produce, and drives home the point that health-conscious vegans don't need to miss out when it comes to gourmet enjoyments.

I think you'll be continually impressed by the quality of the recipes in this book, but there's an entirely other level of significance to *Vive le Vegan!* I've spent many years of my life looking closely at the business of animal agriculture. In my books, I've shown that this is an industry that depends on cruel practices in order to enhance its bottom line. While various animal welfare reforms are achievable and should certainly be sought, the easiest and most reliable way to eat a diet that is free of animal cruelty is to avoid the products of farmed animals altogether.

Many people assume that concerns over cruelty can be addressed by becoming a lacto-ovo vegetarian, and buying free-range eggs and organic milk. Unfortunately, welfare standards for these foods are utterly lacking. And, just as troubling, these foods depend on slaughter every bit as much as their factory farmed counterparts. There is simply no such thing as animal agriculture without suffering and killing – the economics just don't allow it.

Books like this play a decisive role in helping society shift toward cruelty-free eating. In our fast-food culture, people urgently need to be taught the basics of healthy and humane food preparation. This book provides an ideal entry-point into the world of vegan cooking. In these pages, Dreena proves that it doesn't take huge amounts of culinary training to learn how to prepare delicious vegan meals. *Vive le Vegan!* gives you everything you need to get going, all in one fun and inviting book.

While becoming vegan is easy, it does take a little work at the beginning. It's important to spend some time reading about nutrition so you don't inadvertently adapt a diet that is deficient in nutrients. But the real key is to spend a bit of time every day trying new foods, and to keep at it until you've assembled a wealth of dining options that you enjoy. I remember my first few weeks as a vegan, and how exciting it was when I sat down at the table to sample a delicious new recipe. As I chewed I would think, "Veganism isn't difficult at all. It's fun!"

This book offers you that same wonderful, life-affirming experience – an experience that happens whenever great food and compassionate values intersect. Healthy, delicious, and humanely produced food is the foundation of a meaningful life. *Vive les animaux!*

Erik Marcus is the author of Meat Market: Animals, Ethics, and Money *and the publisher of* Vegan.com.

Introduction

For me, there is a strange correlation between cookbooks and pregnancy. In 2001 my first cookbook, *The Everyday Vegan*, was published just six months after my daughter was born. Three years later, my second child and second cookbook are coming into the world the same month. More than coincidence, this is quite appropriate, because it was largely my experience as a vegan mother that led to the creation of the new recipes and information you will find in *Vive le Vegan!*

As a new mom, I discovered new responsibilities. I was (and still am) busier than ever, a fact that affected my meal planning, preparation, and cooking. I also had an increased need to make meals even quicker than before. But I wasn't willing to sacrifice flavor and nutrition.

Once I got my bearings as a mom, I began creating new recipes. The result was a number of delicious, simple, nutritious dishes, but with less manual labor and stovetop attention. I found new ways to create hearty soups, casseroles, entrées, handy snacks, and scrumptious desserts. While there are a few recipes that are best prepared when time is on your side, the majority are fast and easy to make. These dishes are full of flavor and texture, and use fresh produce along with beans, grains, and other pantry items for easy preparation.

I learned more about different grains and beans, and new foods such as hemp, because as my child grew through different stages as a newborn, I wanted to introduce foods that not only packed a nutritional punch, but also promoted her health and development. I also wanted my family to eat more whole grains and beans, and to use different flours in baking, for added variety and nutrition.

This is one of the few cookbooks you will see that features hemp products. Hemp seed nuts and nut butter provide complete protein and essential fatty acids that we can only get from our diet. Hemp seed oil is also rich in the essential fatty acids. More detailed information about hemp products and their nutritional value can be found in the "Hemp Foods" section (p. 169). Manitoba Harvest Hemp Foods and Oils provided all of the hemp foods I used in my recipe testing, as well as the product information outlined in the Hemp Foods section.

Vive le Vegan! contains many recipes that use whole grains such as kamut, brown rice, quinoa, and millet; beans such as adzuki, kidney, navy, and chickpeas (garbanzo beans); flours like spelt, barley, and oat; and few recipes that use soy. I suspect that many vegetarians and vegans rely a little too heavily on soy, and while I sill include it in my family's diet, no one food should be consumed excessively.

There are many wheat-free recipes that call for flours such as spelt, barley, and kamut. These flours provide different nutrients, textures, and flavors to your baking. Even if you don't have a wheat sensitivity, it is important to vary the grains in your diet, so I encourage you to try some of these recipes. Throughout this book, look for recipes marked as wheat-free, as well as others that offer wheat-free options.

I learned a great deal about feeding my daughter as she moved through her baby and toddler years. I was particularly fascinated by information given to me by my doctor, Trang Duong, Registered Midwife and Nauturopathic Physician, about how and when to introduce food to children at different stages through their first three years. I saw this information as invaluable to other parents, so I have included a section entitled "Feeding Your Vegan Baby and Toddler" (p. 139). This section includes a Food Introduction Schedule, which outlines when to introduce certain foods and identifies those that are most allergenic.

Using this schedule as a guide, I created meals for my daughter. In the "Feeding Your Vegan Baby and Toddler" section, I share the tips and techniques I used to prepare food for her. I understand that busy moms and dads do not have much time to work with measured ingredients. The cooking techniques in this section are, therefore, not measured recipes, but rather practical tips and instructions to help you prepare healthy meals and snacks for your children.

One of the most exciting aspects of *Vive le Vegan!* is the contribution of the foreword by Erik Marcus. Erik's writings have educated people about vegan issues including animal rights, health concerns, and environmental impacts. This work has inspired many to make changes for themselves and their surroundings, not only by becoming vegan but also by taking action. If you are new to the vegetarian or vegan lifestyle, visit *Vegan.com* to become more informed about vegan issues and Erik's work.

I truly hope you enjoy this book and discover some new favorite dishes for your family and friends. I love creating recipes and am thrilled to have the opportunity to share some once again. I also love hearing any feedback or questions you have, so please e-mail me through my website at *dreenaburton.com*.

Breakfast

& Brunch

Apple Oat Pancakes

Wheat-Free

Ground oats are a wonderful alternative to flours in many recipes. They work beautifully here with the apples and spices for delightful, wholesome pancakes!

1 cup	ground oats (see Cooking Notes, p. 167)
1 tbsp	baking powder
¼ tsp	cinnamon
⅛ - ¼ tsp	ground cardamom
⅛ tsp	sea salt
1 cup	vanilla non-dairy milk
1 tbsp	canola oil
1	small apple, or ½ large apple, peeled and cored, cut into quarters then thinly sliced (see note)

In a large bowl, add the ground oats and sift in the baking powder. Add the cinnamon, ground cardamom, and salt, and stir through to combine well. In a small bowl, combine the non-dairy milk and canola oil and stir in the sliced apple. Add the wet mixture to the dry mixture and stir through. The mixture will be rather loose at first, so let it sit for a few minutes to thicken.

Heat a lightly oiled skillet over medium-high heat for a few minutes until hot, then reduce heat to low and let it rest for another couple of minutes. Using a ladle, scoop the batter into the skillet to form pancakes. Let cook for a few minutes, until small bubbles start to form on the outer edge of the pancakes and then the center. Check the bottom to see if it is golden brown, then flip to cook the other side, for a couple of minutes. As you work through the batter, it will thicken further. If desired, add a touch more milk about halfway through the batter to thin it out slightly, or spread out the batter more when ladling onto the skillet. Serve with pure maple syrup, Blueberry Maple Syrup (p. 20), or a fruit sauce.

Makes 6-8 medium to large pancakes.

Pear is a fine substitution for the apple in this recipe. However, ripe pears are moister, and you may need to add another 1-2 tablespoons of ground oats to thicken the batter.

Banana Bliss Pancakes

These are satisfying pancakes with the natural sweetness of banana. Perfect on a cool morning, or even as comfort food for dinner!

1 cup	**whole-wheat pastry flour**
1 tbsp	**baking powder**
¼ tsp	**cinnamon**
⅛ tsp	**freshly grated nutmeg**
⅛ tsp	**sea salt**
1 cup + 1 tbsp	**vanilla non-dairy milk**
1 tbsp	**canola oil**
1	**medium ripe banana, sliced**

In a large bowl, add the flour and sift in the baking powder. Add the cinnamon, nutmeg, and salt, and stir through to combine well. In a small bowl, combine the non-dairy milk and canola oil and stir through. Add the wet mixture to the dry mixture and stir through, until just well combined, adding the banana slices as it comes together.

Heat a lightly oiled skillet over medium-high heat for a few minutes until hot, then reduce heat to low and let it rest for another couple of minutes. Using a ladle, scoop the batter into the skillet to form pancakes. Let cook for a few minutes, until small bubbles start to form on the outer edge of the pancakes and then the center. Check the bottom to see if it is golden brown, then flip to cook the other side, for a couple of minutes. Serve with pure maple syrup, Blueberry Maple Syrup (p. 20), or a fruit sauce.

Makes 6-8 medium to large pancakes.

Blueberry Maple Syrup

Wheat-Free

A simple recipe that makes maple syrup for pancakes and waffles an even bigger treat!

1 cup	**frozen or fresh blueberries (see note)**
½ cup	**maple syrup**

In a saucepan over low heat, add the blueberries. Cover and let cook until the berries have softened and somewhat dissolved. Remove from heat and add the maple syrup. With a handblender or in a blender, purée the mixture a little, smoothing to desired consistency. Cool to room temperature and serve. Extra syrup can be refrigerated for a couple of weeks, or frozen to be thawed for later use.

You can use other berries in this recipe if you like, such as raspberries or strawberries.

If you want to give the syrup a little zing and freshness, add a squeeze or two of fresh lemon juice when you add the maple syrup.

Cinnamon Sweet Hemp Spread

Wheat-Free

Kids will love this sweet spread! Try it on bread, waffles, pancakes, crackers, or apple slices, mashed with banana for a sandwich filling, or stirred into warm cereal.

½ cup	**hemp seed nut butter (see note)**
1½ - 2 tbsp	**pure maple syrup**
1 tsp	**cinnamon**

In a bowl, combine all the ingredients and stir through until well combined. Use as desired on bread, etc., and refrigerate remainder in an airtight container.

You can try these flavorings with other seed and nut butters as well, such as almond butter or peanut butter.

Creamy Raspberry Oatmeal

Wheat-Free

Who doesn't love creamy oatmeal on a cool morning? Try this version with the fresh and vibrant flavor of raspberries to perk up ordinary oatmeal.

1 cup	rolled oats
1½ cups	vanilla non-dairy milk
1 cup	water
⅛ tsp	sea salt
⅛ tsp	freshly grated nutmeg
⅛ tsp	allspice
⅓ - ½ cup	frozen raspberries (or other frozen berries)
1 tbsp	maple syrup (optional)

In a saucepan over medium-high heat, combine all the ingredients except the maple syrup and bring to a boil, stirring occasionally. Reduce heat to low and let simmer covered for 14-15 minutes or a little longer if needed, stirring occasionally, until the liquid is absorbed. Stir in the frozen raspberries, until they have dissolved a little. Taste, and if desired, add the maple syrup to sweeten. Serve, topped with an extra drizzle of milk and maple syrup, if desired.

Makes 3-4 servings.

Want to enhance the nutritional value of this oatmeal even more? Try stirring in a tablespoon or two of flax meal or hemp seed nuts when serving (don't cook it with the oatmeal). You could also stir in a little nut butter, like cashew butter, while the oatmeal is still warm.

Fantastic French Toast

Wheat-Free Option

Growing up, my husband and I both loved French toast. We also love this recipe because the combination of flax meal and tofu give a texture similar to an egg batter for a traditional tasting – better tasting, actually – French toast!

1 cup	**vanilla non-dairy milk**
2 tbsp	**flax meal**
½ cup	**silken firm tofu**
¼ tsp	**cinnamon**
⅛ tsp	**freshly grated nutmeg**
⅛ tsp	**sea salt**
1 tsp	**canola oil**
8 - 9 slices	**bread of choice (see note)**
2 - 3 tsp	**canola oil (or more, if needed, for frying)**

Using a handblender or in a blender, purée the non-dairy milk, flax meal, tofu, cinnamon, nutmeg, salt, and canola oil until very smooth and thick (it will get thicker as it sits a little while and the flax absorbs some of the liquid). Dip a slice of bread in the batter. Turn over and let it sit for a few moments to soak, then remove and place on a plate until ready to fry.

In a skillet over medium-high heat, add the canola oil when hot and reduce heat to low/medium-low. Fry bread for 4-6 minutes on each side, until lightly brown (try to flip only once so that the batter will set and brown nicely on the bread). Serve with pure maple syrup.

Makes 3-4 servings.

While whole-grain breads are certainly healthier, white bread is traditionally used for French toast. Sometimes the earthy, nutty quality of the whole-grain breads can overpower the flavor of the batter, but it will still taste good, so use whatever you like.

For a wheat-free option, use a white spelt bread (or whole-grain spelt or kamut bread).

Hemp Power Shake

Wheat-Free

This recipe makes a thick, tasty shake that gets its protein from hemp instead of soy protein powders. Many of us love protein shakes, but want some alternatives to soy, whether to diversify our diets or because of allergies. I like to use plain non-dairy milk, since the overripe banana adds sweetness, but you can use a flavored variety if you like.

1 cup	plain, vanilla, or chocolate non-dairy milk
½ cup	frozen overripe banana, cut in chunks
1½ - 2 tbsp	hemp seed nut butter
	or
¼ - ⅓ cup	hemp seed nuts
	or
1 tbsp	hemp protein powder

With a handblender or in a blender, combine all the ingredients and purée until smooth.

Makes 1 generous shake or 2 small.

Millet-Amaranth Porridge

Wheat-Free

A lightly spiced cereal that's somewhat like a rice pudding. Sweeten chilled leftovers and top with a little soy yogurt or ice cream for a treat for your kids (or you)!

2½ cups	water
¾ cup	millet, rinsed
¼ cup	amaranth
½ tsp	cinnamon
⅛ tsp	sea salt
few pinches	ground cardamom
few pinches	allspice
1 cup	plain or vanilla non-dairy milk (see note)
¼ - ⅓ cup	raisins or chopped dried apricots

In a saucepan over medium-high heat, combine the water, millet, amaranth, cinnamon, sea salt, cardamom, and allspice and bring to a boil, stirring occasionally. Reduce heat to low, cover, and cook for 18-20 minutes. Stir in the non-dairy milk and raisins or dried apricots. Increase the heat to medium-low, cover and cook for another 8-10 minutes, stirring occasionally. At this point, the porridge should be thick and soft with most of the liquid absorbed. To thicken it further, let it cook without a lid for another few minutes. If desired, use a handblender to purée the porridge a bit in spots, to make it smoother. Otherwise, remove from heat and serve, sweetening to taste with maple syrup if desired and stirring in additional non-dairy milk to desired consistency.

Makes 4-5 servings.

If using plain milk, you may want to add a little sweetener to your porridge along with the milk, such as 1-2 tablespoons of maple syrup.

For an additional nutritional boost, when serving, stir in a little flax meal and/or hemp seed nuts.

Orange Mango Smoothie

Wheat-Free

A smooth, refreshing drink that's especially nice in the spring and summer. Boost the nutritional value with some hemp protein powder if you like!

1 cup	**good quality orange juice**
½ cup	**overripe banana, sliced or in chunks, fresh or frozen**
⅓ cup	**cubed mango, fresh or frozen (see note)**
1 - 1½ tsp	**freshly squeezed lemon juice**
1 tbsp	**hemp protein powder (optional)**
¼ cup	**ice cubes (optional)**

With a handblender or in a blender, combine all the ingredients and purée until smooth.

Makes 1 generous smoothie or 2 small.

When mangoes are abundant and ripe in the spring and summer, cut several into chunks and store in small portions. They're great for blending into smoothies or ice creams, or using in fruit crisps!

Portobello Bagel Melt

Wheat-Free
Option

The toppings on this bagel are warm and well-seasoned, and will almost melt in your mouth. Great for a relaxed weekend morning!

1	large portobello mushroom, woody stem removed, cleaned and thickly sliced (see note)
2 tsp	extra-virgin olive oil
1 tbsp	vegetarian Worcestershire sauce
few pinches	sea salt
few pinches	freshly ground black pepper
1	whole-grain bagel (or bagel of choice), sliced in half
½ cup	(packed) baby spinach, or regular spinach, torn or roughly chopped
3 - 4 tbsp	green onions, roughly chopped (green portion only)
⅓ - ½ cup	mozzarella-style VeganRella or other non-dairy cheese, grated
1 - 1½ tbsp	extra-virgin olive oil (to finish)

Preheat oven to broil. In a bowl, combine the mushrooms, olive oil, and Worcestershire sauce and toss well. Place the mushrooms on a baking sheet lined with parchment paper, and sprinkle with sea salt and pepper. Place under the broiler (on high rack) for 5 6 minutes, flipping once, until just browned. While mushrooms are grilling, lightly toast the bagel halves.

When mushrooms are done, remove and set oven to bake at 425°F (218°C) (and lower the rack if necessary). On the same baking sheet lined with parchment paper, place the bagels, arrange the spinach on top (sprinkle with a pinch of sea salt), followed by the mushrooms, green onions, and the VeganRella. Bake for 7-9 minutes, until cheese is melted. Remove and finish with a drizzle of olive oil. Serve as is or with ketchup or other condiments.

Makes 1 or 2 servings, with accompaniments.

For a wheat-free option, use wheat-free bagels and substitute tamari in place of the Worcestershire sauce.

You can use other veggies instead of mushrooms or spinach such as roasted red peppers, fresh tomato slices, or zucchini (grill zucchini as you would the mushrooms).

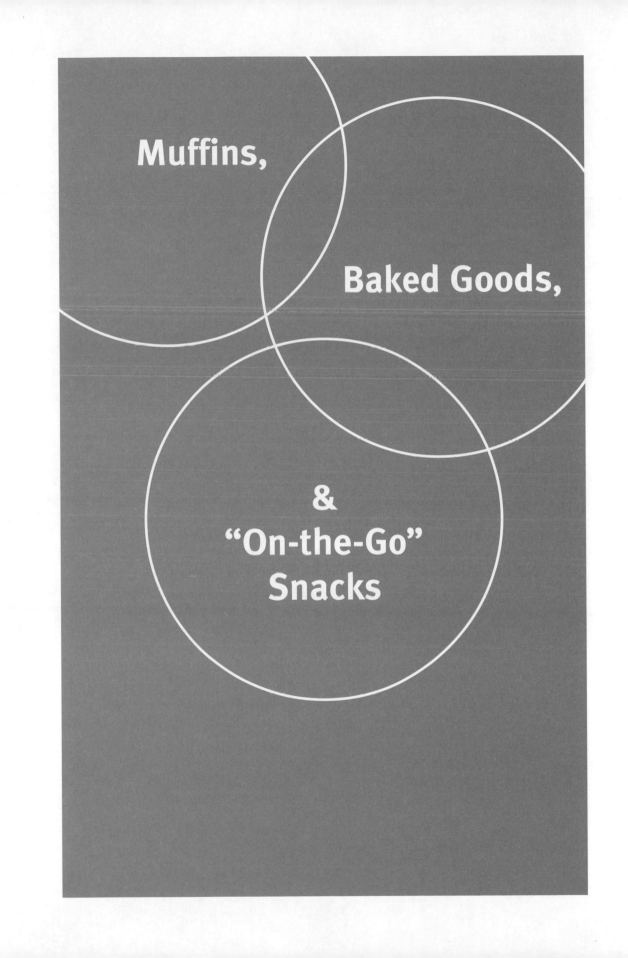

Muffins,

Baked Goods,

&
"On-the-Go"
Snacks

Apple-Hemp Muffins

Moist, lightly spiced muffins with the added nutrition of hemp seed nuts. These are easy and quick, and sure to please both kids and adults!

1½ cups	whole-wheat pastry flour
1 cup	ground oats (see Cooking Notes, p. 167)
½ cup	hemp seed nuts
2 tsp	baking powder
1 tsp	baking soda
¼ tsp	sea salt
½ tsp	cinnamon
¼ tsp	freshly grated nutmeg
⅛ tsp	ground cardamom
1 cup	unsweetened applesauce
½ cup	pure maple syrup
¾ cup	plain non-dairy milk
1 tsp	pure vanilla extract
3 - 3½ tbsp	canola oil

Preheat oven to 350°F (176°C). In a large bowl, combine the dry ingredients, sifting in the baking powder and baking soda. Stir through until well combined. In another bowl, combine applesauce, maple syrup, non-dairy milk, vanilla, and canola oil, and mix together. Add the wet mixture to the dry mixture, and gently fold and mix through, until just combined (do not overmix). Spoon the mixture into a muffin pan lined with cupcake liners, or lightly oiled. Bake for 25-30 minutes (less time for smaller muffins, longer for larger), until a toothpick inserted in the center comes out clean.

Makes 8 medium-large muffins or 12 small muffins.

Apricot-Almond Loaf

Wheat-Free

A mellow snack loaf with dried apricots and toasted almonds speckled throughout. Lovely in the morning or afternoon with herbal tea!

½ cup	ground oats (see Cooking Notes, p. 167)
½ cup	unrefined sugar
⅓ cup	toasted almond slivers (see Cooking Notes, p. 167)
1¼ cup	spelt flour (see note)
⅓ cup	barley flour (see note)
1½ tsp	baking powder
1 tsp	baking soda
¼ tsp	freshly grated nutmeg
¼ tsp	sea salt
1 cup	plain or vanilla non-dairy milk
1 tbsp	flax meal
½ cup	applesauce
⅓ - ½ cup	dried apricots, chopped
1 tsp	pure vanilla extract
½ tsp	almond extract
2½ tbsp	canola oil
¼ cup	toasted almond slivers (garnish)

Preheat oven to 350°F (176°C). In a large bowl, combine the oats, sugar, almonds, nutmeg, and sea salt, and sift in the flours, baking powder, and baking soda. In another bowl, combine the milk with the flax meal and stir through. Add the applesauce, apricots, vanilla and almond extracts, and canola oil and mix well. Add the wet mixture to the dry mixture, stirring through until just well combined. Pour mixture into a lightly oiled loaf pan. Sprinkle remaining almond slices down the centre of the loaf, patting them in lightly. Bake for 40-45 minutes, or until golden and a toothpick inserted in the center comes out clean. Cool and cut into thick slices.

Makes 8-9 slices.

You can substitute the spelt and barley flours with unbleached all-purpose flour or whole-wheat pastry flour (or a combination of both). If so, use only 1 cup of flour in place of the 1¼ cup of spelt.

Banana Oat Bundles

Wheat-Free

A cross between a cookie and a mini-muffin, these bundles are a tasty, wholesome treat that are fast to prepare and can be enjoyed hot from the oven, or cooled to pack in lunches!

1 cup	**quick oats**
1 cup	**ground oats (see Cooking Notes, p. 167)**
¼ cup	**unrefined sugar**
¼ tsp	**sea salt**
¼ tsp	**cinnamon or ground cardamon**
¼ tsp	**nutmeg**
1 tsp	**baking powder**
1 cup	**overripe banana, puréed (roughly 2 large bananas) (see note)**
1 tsp	**pure vanilla extract**
3 - 3½ tbsp	**canola oil**

Preheat oven to 350°F (176°C). In a large bowl, combine the oats, ground oats, sugar, sea salt, cinnamon, and nutmeg, and sift in the baking powder. Stir through until well combined. In another bowl, combine the puréed banana, vanilla, and canola oil, stirring through. Add the wet mixture to the dry mixture, and stir through until just well combined. Drop large spoonfuls onto a baking sheet lined with parchment paper. Bake for 12-15 minutes, until lightly golden. Remove from oven and let cool on pan for 1 minute, then transfer to a cooling rack.

Makes 12-15 bundles.

Use a food processor or blender to purée the bananas. It produces a smooth, almost liquefied texture, which takes a long time to achieve by mashing.

Try adding about ⅓ cup of toasted nuts (see Cooking Notes, p. 167) such as walnuts or cashews to these cookies; alternatively, some dried fruit, or chocolate or carob chips.

Blueberry Bounty Buns

These buns burst with blueberry goodness! A cross between a muffin and a scone, they're just sweet enough, and very easy to make.

1 cup + 1 tbsp	**ground oats (see Cooking Notes, p. 167)**
1 cup	**whole wheat pastry flour or unbleached all-purpose flour (see note)**
1½ tsp	**baking powder**
½ tsp	**baking soda**
¼ cup	**unrefined sugar**
½ tsp	**cinnamon (or freshly grated nutmeg)**
¼ tsp	**sea salt**
¾ cup	**vanilla non-dairy milk**
1 tbsp	**flax meal**
2 tbsp	**pure maple syrup**
1 tsp	**pure vanilla extract**
¼ cup	**canola oil**
1 cup	**frozen or fresh blueberries**

Preheat oven to 350°F (176°C). In a large bowl, combine the ground oats and flour, and sift in the baking powder and baking soda. Stir in the remaining dry ingredients and mix to combine well. In another bowl, combine the non-dairy milk and flax meal, stir and let sit for 1 minute. Add the maple syrup, vanilla, and canola oil, and stir through. Add the blueberries. Immediately add the wet mixture to the dry mixture, and stir through until just well combined. Scoop large spoonfuls of the mixture (roughly ½ cup each) onto a baking sheet lined with parchment paper. Bake for 20-23 minutes, until the buns are lightly golden and are set in the center (gently touch to check). Remove from oven and let cool on pan for 1 minute, then transfer to a cooling rack.

Makes 6-7 buns.

For a wheat-free version, use spelt flour instead, but add an extra 3 tablespoons in addition to the 1 cup.

Carob Chip Muffins

Wheat-Free

These muffins are so yummy – they have that cake-like sweetness and moist texture, and when still warm, the carob chips are softly melted. All this, and they're healthy too!

2 cups	barley flour
½ cup	unrefined sugar
⅓ - ½ cup	carob chips
¼ cup	unsweetened shredded coconut
¼ tsp	sea salt
1 - 2 tsp	orange zest (from 1 orange)
1 tbsp	baking powder
½ tsp	baking soda
¼ - ½ tsp	freshly grated nutmeg
1 cup	plain non-dairy milk
3 tbsp	pure maple syrup
1½ tsp	pure vanilla extract
⅓ cup	canola oil

Preheat oven to 375°F (190°C). In a large bowl, combine the dry ingredients, sifting in the baking powder and baking soda. Stir through until well combined. In another bowl, combine the non-dairy milk, maple syrup, vanilla, and canola oil. Add the wet mixture to the dry mixture, and gently fold and mix through, until just combined. Spoon the mixture into a muffin pan lined with cupcake liners, or lightly oiled. Bake for 21-24 minutes (baking time depends on size of muffin), until a toothpick inserted in the center comes out clean.

Makes 7-9 muffins.

Choco-Cinna-Nut Biscotti

A fun twist on biscotti for a chocolate treat that's not too sweet!

2 cups	**unbleached all-purpose flour**
⅔ cup	**unrefined sugar**
⅓ cup	**cocoa powder**
¾ tsp	**cinnamon**
2 tsp	**baking powder**
½ tsp	**baking soda**
¼ tsp	**sea salt**
½ - ¾ cup	**toasted nuts (e.g., pecans, almond slivers, walnuts) (see Cooking Notes, p. 167)**
¼ - ⅓ cup	**non-dairy chocolate chips (espresso-flavored are good)**
½ cup	**pure maple syrup**
⅓ cup	**water**
1 tsp	**pure vanilla extract**
1 tsp	**mocha extract (or ½ tsp almond extract)**
⅓ cup	**canola oil**
1½ - 2 tbsp	**unrefined sugar (garnish)**

Preheat oven to 350°F (176°C). In a large bowl, combine the dry ingredients, sifting in the flour, cocoa powder, baking powder, and baking soda. In another bowl, combine the maple syrup, water, vanilla and mocha extracts, and canola oil. Add the wet mixture to the dry mixture, and mix until well combined, making a thick dough. Divide the dough in half, and shape into logs (roughly 1" thick, 4" wide, and 8-9" long). Place on a baking sheet lined with parchment paper (make sure there is space between them), and bake for 35-37 minutes. Remove from oven to let cool, about 10 minutes (see note).

Using a serrated knife, cut biscotti strips on a slight diagonal, about 1½" thick. Sprinkle with the unrefined sugar and bake for another 12-20 minutes (less time for chewier cookies, longer for crispier ones). Remove from oven and let cool.

Makes 12 or more biscotti.

Leave the biscotti logs on the baking tray to cool on top of a cooling rack so they can be easily sliced before baking again. When cooling the biscotti slices, you can again leave them on the tray on top of a cooling rack. Note that they will be crispier than if transferred directly to the cooling rack.

Dip the ends of the biscotti cookies in good-quality melted non-dairy chocolate and let cool on a baking tray lined with parchment paper.

Diane's Stork Muffins

Wheat-Free

When my daughter was born, my sister delivered a batch of these delicious, nutritious "baby" muffins, and did I ever appreciate them! Being hungrier than ever because of breastfeeding, these little muffins were (and are) great healthy snacks!

2 cups	ground oats (see Cooking Notes, p. 167)
½ cup	barley flour (see note)
½ cup	kamut flour (see note)
¾ cup	unsweetened shredded coconut
1 tbsp	baking powder
1 tsp	baking soda
2 - 2½ tsp	cinnamon
½ tsp	freshly grated nutmeg
¾ cup	pitted dates, chopped
½ cup	dried cranberries
½ tsp	sea salt (little scant)
2 tbsp	flax meal
1¼ cups	plain non-dairy milk
½ cup	pure maple syrup
2 tsp	almond extract
1 tsp	pure vanilla extract
⅓ cup	canola oil

Preheat oven to 350°F (176°C). In a large bowl, combine the dry ingredients except the flax meal, sifting in the flours, baking powder, and baking soda. Stir through until well combined. In another bowl, combine the flax meal and the milk. Add the maple syrup, extracts, and canola oil and stir through. Add the wet mixture to the dry mixture, and stir through until well combined (the batter will thicken as the oats absorb the liquid). Spoon the mixture into two muffin pans lined with cupcake liners or lightly oiled. Bake for 16-18 minutes, or until a toothpick inserted in the center comes out clean. Remove from oven, let cool for 1 minute, then transfer to a cooling rack.

Makes 18-20 small muffins.

You can substitute the kamut and barley flours with whole-wheat pastry flour if desired.

Easy Pleasin' Oat Bars

Wheat-Free

These are wonderful snack bars that are a little crunchy, a little chewy, and not too sweet. They're a cinch to make, and also freeze well!

2 cups	**ground oats (see Cooking Notes, p. 167) (see note)**
1 cup	**quick oats**
¼ tsp	**sea salt**
¼ tsp	**cinnamon**
¼ cup	**pure maple syrup**
⅓ cup	**fruit sweetener or other thick honey alternative**
¼ cup	**vanilla or plain non-dairy milk**
1½ - 2 tbsp	**canola oil**

Preheat oven to 350°F (176°C). In a large bowl, combine all the dry ingredients. Add the wet ingredients into the dry mixture, stirring until well combined. Transfer the mixture to a lightly oiled 8"x12" baking dish and press it down until evenly distributed. Using a sharp knife, cut to mark out the bars before you bake them to make it easier to fully cut and remove the bars once baked. (I usually mark out 12 rectangular bars, but you can make whatever size you like.) Bake for 19-21 minutes, then remove and let cool in pan. Once cool, use a sharp knife to fully cut the bars, then remove with a spatula.

Makes 10-14 bars (depending on how they are cut).

You can substitute ½ cup or more of the ground oats with ½ cup or more of hemp seed nuts.

For some different flavors and textures, try stirring in ¼ cup of dried fruits and/or toasted nuts (see Cooking Notes, p. 167), such as dried cranberries and toasted pecans, raisins and toasted almonds, dried apricots and toasted walnuts, etc. Other additions to consider are sliced bananas, or chocolate or carob chips.

Energy Cookies

Wheat-Free

These treats are full of natural goodness and just enough sweetness to be called cookies. Pack them in lunches, or take them on outings, hikes, or whenever you need an energy pick-me-up!

½ cup + 1 tbsp	barley flour
¼ cup	spelt flour
½ tsp	baking powder
½ cup	sunflower seeds
¼ cup	hemp seed nuts
¼ cup	pumpkin seeds
¼ cup	raisins or other dried fruit, chopped
3 - 4 tbsp	non-dairy chocolate chips or carob chips
1 tsp	cinnamon
¼ tsp	sea salt
2 tbsp	flax meal
¼ cup	pure maple syrup
2 tbsp	non-dairy milk
1 - 1½ tsp	blackstrap molasses
1 tsp	pure vanilla extract
3 tbsp	canola oil

Preheat oven to 350°F (176°C). In a large bowl, combine all dry ingredients except the flax meal, mixing well. In another bowl, combine the flax meal with the maple syrup and milk, and stir through. Add the molasses, vanilla, and canola oil and stir through. Add the wet mixture to the dry mixture and stir through until well combined. Drop spoonfuls of the batter (about 2 tbsp each) on a baking sheet lined with parchment paper. Flatten a little and bake for 13-14 minutes. Remove from oven and let cool for 1 minute on sheet, then transfer to a cooling rack.

Makes 10-12 cookies.

Orange-Poppy Seed Muffins

Wheat-Free

My daughter calls muffins "mommy cakes," and this recipe is a favorite for her. Not most kids' definition of "cake," but I like that she considers muffins such a treat … at least for now!

1¼ cup	ground oats (see Cooking Notes, p. 167)
2 tbsp	poppy seeds
2 tbsp	unrefined sugar
1 - 2 tsp	orange zest (from 1 orange)
¼ tsp	sea salt
½ tsp	cinnamon
⅛ tsp	allspice (or ¼ tsp freshly grated nutmeg)
1 cup	barley flour (or unbleached all-purpose flour)
2 tsp	baking powder
1 tsp	baking soda
¼ cup	freshly squeezed or good quality orange juice (roughly 1 medium orange, squeezed)
1½ tbsp	flax meal
1 cup	unsweetened applesauce
⅓ cup	plain non-dairy milk
⅓ cup	pure maple syrup
1 tsp	pure vanilla extract
3 tbsp	canola oil

Preheat oven to 375°F (190°C). In a large bowl, combine the ground oats, poppy seeds, sugar, orange zest, sea salt, cinnamon, and allspice, and sift in the flour, baking powder and baking soda. Stir through until well combined. In another bowl, combine the orange juice with the flax meal and stir through. Add the applesauce, non-dairy milk, maple syrup, vanilla, and canola oil. Add the wet mixture to the dry mixture, and stir through until well combined. Spoon the mixture into a muffin pan lined with cupcake liners. Bake for 22-25 minutes (baking time depends on size of muffin), until a toothpick inserted in the center comes out clean.

Makes 8-9 medium-large muffins or 10-12 small.

Squirrelly "Scones"

Wheat-Free

These "scones" are not made the traditional way, but they look like them. Packed with nuts, seeds, and fruit, they're satisfying and super-healthy!

1 cup	ground oats (see Cooking Notes, p. 167)
1 cup	barley flour (or unbleached all-purpose flour or whole wheat pastry flour)
1½ tsp	baking powder
½ tsp	baking soda
½ cup	toasted pecans (or other nuts) (see Cooking Notes, p. 167)
⅓ cup	pumpkin seeds
¼ cup	sunflower seeds
⅓ cup	raisins
¼ cup	non-dairy chocolate chips (or carob chips or more dried fruit) (optional)
¼ cup	unrefined sugar
½ - ¾ tsp	cinnamon
¼ tsp	sea salt
1½ tbsp	flax meal
¾ cup	vanilla or plain non-dairy milk
3 tbsp	pure maple syrup
1 tsp	pure vanilla extract
3 - 4 tbsp	canola oil

Preheat oven to 350°F (176°C). In a large bowl, combine all the dry ingredients except the flax meal, sifting in the flour, baking powder, and baking soda. In another bowl, combine the flax meal with the non-dairy milk and stir through. Add the maple syrup, vanilla, and canola oil and stir through. Add the wet mixture to the dry mixture and mix until well combined. The mixture may be a little loose at first, but will thicken as the flour and oats absorb the liquid. Let it rest for a minute, then drop large spoonfuls of the mixture (roughly ½ cup each) onto a baking sheet lined with parchment paper. Bake for 20-24 minutes, until golden and a toothpick inserted in center comes out clean. Remove from oven, let cool on pan for 1 minute, then transfer to a cooling rack.

Makes 6-7 "scones."

Totally Nutty Bars

Wheat-Free

I created these bars as an alternative to most energy snack bars that use some type of grain as the base. With just nuts, seeds, dried fruit, and natural sweeteners, these bars will boost your energy with crunchy, chewy goodness. They keep well in the freezer, so make a few batches and store in an airtight container for snacks on-the-run.

1 cup	sunflower seeds
½ cup	pumpkin seeds
½ cup	toasted pecans (see Cooking Notes, p. 167) (see note)
½ cup	toasted almond slivers (see Cooking Notes, p. 167) (see note)
¼ cup	hemp seed nuts or sesame seeds, or combination (see note)
¼ - ⅓ cup	raisins or dried apricots, chopped
3 tbsp	flax meal
¼ - ⅓ cup	thick honey alternative (e.g., brown rice syrup or barley malt)
2 tbsp	cashew or almond butter
½ - 1 tsp	blackstrap molasses
¼ tsp	cinnamon
⅛ tsp	sea salt

In a large bowl, combine the seeds, nuts, raisins, and flax meal. In a saucepan over medium-low heat, combine the honey alternative, cashew or almond butter, molasses, cinnamon, and salt. Stir until it is just heated through and well combined (do not boil). Remove from heat and immediately add to the dry mixture. Stir through well, then transfer to a lightly oiled 8"x12" baking dish (or smaller dish for thicker bars). Press the mixture down into the dish until evenly distributed (use a small piece of parchment paper to help press it down). Refrigerate until completely cooled, then cut into squares or rectangular bars. If you freeze some, be sure to separate the layers with parchment paper so they don't stick.

Makes 10-12 bars (depending on how they are cut).

You can use other toasted nuts, such as cashews or walnuts. Alternatively, if you want to use more hemp and/or sesame seeds instead, go right ahead! The hemp seed nuts are really delicious in these bars.

Vinaigrettes, Sauces, & Toppings

Balsamic-Garlic Flax Oil

This recipe is a pleasant and convenient way to include flax oil in your daily diet. My family always enjoys the balsamic/olive oil dips at restaurants that you can dredge good breads in. I was preparing such a dip at home one night but decided to try flax oil instead of olive. It was okay, until I added garlic – not a lot, just a hint to give it more flavor and mask any bitterness in the flax oil. We now have this every night with our meals, either drizzled on our main course or as a dip with bread.

¼ **cup**	**balsamic vinegar**
1	**large clove garlic, cut into 3 or 4 slices**
½ **cup**	**flax oil (see note)**

In a bowl or jar, combine the vinegar and the garlic. Let sit for about 15 minutes to infuse the vinegar with the garlic flavor. Add the flax oil, and refrigerate for 10-15 minutes or more before using.

If you have any left over, you may want to remove the garlic before refrigerating for the next day; the longer the garlic steeps in the oil and vinegar, the stronger the flavor. If you leave it in and find it is too strong, you can always add extra oil and vinegar to dilute it a little. Also, the garlic can spoil in the oil after time, so it is best to use within a few days and then make a fresh batch.

Since hemp seed oil is such an incredible source of essential fatty acids, you can also use it in place of some or all of the flax oil. It will give a nuttier flavor and a beautiful green color!

Citrus Mint Vinaigrette

Wheat-Free

This is a light and refreshing dressing that is delightful with a heavier and/or spicy main course!

3 tbsp	freshly squeezed lemon or lime juice
1 tbsp	apple cider vinegar or rice vinegar
2 tbsp	fresh mint leaves, torn from stems (no need to chop)
1 - 1½ tsp	lemon or lime zest
1	small clove garlic
3 - 3½ tbsp	pure maple syrup (adjust to taste)
1 tsp	Dijon mustard
½ tsp	sea salt
	freshly ground black pepper to taste
¼ cup	extra-virgin olive oil
2 tbsp	hemp seed oil (or more olive oil)

With a handblender or in a blender, combine all of the ingredients except the oil(s) and purée. Continue blending and drizzle in the oil. Season to taste with additional sea salt and freshly ground black pepper, if desired.

Creamy Avocado Cashew Sauce

Wheat-Free

I love this sauce – it's velvety smooth and cool, and pairs famously with spicy or Mexican inspired dishes such as Chipotle Veggie-Bean Burritos (p. 90).

¾ - 1 cup	plain non-dairy milk (adjust amount to desired consistency)
½ cup	avocado (roughly ½ good-sized avocado)
1 tbsp	cashew butter
2 tbsp	freshly squeezed lemon juice (see note)
½ tsp	sea salt
	freshly ground black pepper (optional)

With a handblender or in a blender, combine all the ingredients (start with ¾ cup of the milk), and purée until very smooth. Adjust to taste with additional sea salt and fresh ground black pepper, if desired, and adjust the consistency of the sauce with more milk, to your preference (the sauce is good both thick and thin!).

If you don't have fresh lemons, you can substitute some apple cider vinegar or rice vinegar, but you won't need as much, about 1½ tbsp.

Creamy Orange-Poppy Seed Dressing

Wheat-Free

This delicious, mild, creamy dressing is particularly nice on spinach salads, or as a cooling topping/dip alongside a spicy main course.

¾ cup	soft tofu
⅓ cup	freshly squeezed or good quality orange juice
3 - 4 tsp	apple cider vinegar or seasoned rice vinegar
1	small clove garlic (optional)
2 - 2½ tsp	honey alternative (see note)
2 tsp	Dijon mustard
½ tsp	sea salt
2 - 3 tbsp	extra-virgin olive oil
2 - 3 tbsp	poppy seeds

With a handblender or in a blender, combine all the ingredients except the oil and poppy seeds, and purée until very smooth. Drizzle in the olive oil and purée again until smooth and thickened. Transfer to a jar or bowl, and stir in the poppy seeds.

Depending on the sweetness of your orange juice, you can use more or less sweetener to taste. Pure maple syrup works well, but you can use any liquid sweetener of choice.

Cumin Lime Vinaigrette

Wheat-Free

This salad dressing pairs wonderfully with Mexican-inspired entrées such as Chipotle Veggie-Bean Burritos (p. 90). A simple salad of greens and some chopped jicama is a great accompaniment.

¼ cup	freshly squeezed lime juice
1	small clove garlic, chopped
2 - 3 tbsp	pure maple syrup (adjust sweetness to taste)
2 tbsp	honey alternative
½ tsp	Dijon mustard
½ tsp	sea salt
¼ tsp	cumin (a little scant)
⅛ tsp	cinnamon
3 tbsp	extra-virgin olive oil
2 - 3 tbsp	sunflower oil or hemp seed oil (or more olive oil)

With a handblender or in a blender, combine all the ingredients except the oil(s) and purée. Continue blending and drizzle in the oil. Season to taste with additional sea salt and freshly ground black pepper, if desired.

Ginger Dipping Sauce

Wheat-Free

This sauce adds kick to vegan spring and egg rolls and is a snap to make. It's also great on the Pumpkin Seed-Coated Lentil Patties (p. 98), or the Moroccan Chickpea Patties (p. 97).

¼ cup	**apple cider vinegar**
4 - 5 tbsp	**pure maple syrup or other honey alternative (or more to taste)**
2½ - 3 tbsp	**tamari**
1 - 1½ tsp	**freshly grated ginger**
1½ tsp	**toasted sesame oil**
¼ tsp	**red pepper flakes (use more or less to taste) (optional)**

In a bowl, combine all the ingredients and stir to mix well until the honey alternative is dissolved. (If needed, warm the sauce a little by placing it in a hot water bath for a few minutes or heating it in the microwave for a few seconds.)

The longer the sauce sits, the more heat it takes on from the ginger and red pepper flakes.

Hemp Sprinkle

Wheat-Free

Use this protein-rich seasoning for salads, pastas, pizzas, soups, sandwiches – anything you like!

1 cup	**hemp seed nuts (or ½ cup hemp seed nut and ½ cup dry roasted pumpkin seeds) (see note)**
¼ tsp	**sea salt**
⅛ tsp	**freshly grated nutmeg**

In a blender or a food processor, combine all the ingredients and pulse/purée until crumbly (do not over-purée, or the mixture will start to turn to nut butter!).

If using roasted pumpkin seeds, you don't need the salt, since the seeds are usually seasoned already. You can omit the nutmeg as well.

Lemon Zinger Vinaigrette

Wheat-Free

This vinaigrette is great with a richer-tasting meal that can really benefit from the tartness and acidity of the lemons. I like tossing it with a simple salad of fresh spinach, chopped green onion, slivered bell peppers, and chopped avocado. It's also nice drizzled on entrées with a starchy component or cooked potatoes.

¼ cup	freshly squeezed lemon juice
2 tbsp	good quality apple juice
3 - 3½ tbsp	honey alternative or pure maple syrup
½ tsp	sea salt (generous)
2½ tsp	Dijon mustard
1	very small clove garlic
1 tsp	tamari
	freshly ground black pepper to taste
¼ cup	hemp seed oil (or more olive oil)
2 - 3 tbsp	extra-virgin olive oil

With a handblender or in a blender, combine all the ingredients except the oils and purée. Continue blending and drizzle in the oils. Season to taste with additional sea salt and freshly ground black pepper, if desired.

Omega Ketchup

Wheat-Free

Turn ordinary ketchup into something more nutritious with the addition of Omega-3 and -6 essential fatty acids. Kids will have it on their veggie burgers and home fries and never know the difference (and you may not either)!

¼ - ⅓ cup	**good quality ketchup**
3 tbsp	**flax oil or hemp seed oil (see note)**

In a bowl, combine the ketchup and oil. Stir or whisk through to emulsify. It will separate some after sitting in the bowl, but you simply need to give it a good stir again.

If you have Balsamic-Garlic Flax Oil (p. 44) on hand, use it as the oil for this recipe. Even a tablespoon, when combined with the ketchup and unflavored flax/hemp seed oil, will make it tastier with its garlicky tones.

Pine-kin Topping

Wheat-Free

A tasty topping that can be sprinkled on salads, soups, pastas, or in sandwiches for extra protein and textural crunch. Just a quick whiz in your food processor (or mini-processor if you have one), and it's ready to use and store in the refrigerator!

½ cup	roasted pumpkin seeds (see note)
⅓ cup	toasted pine nuts (see note)

In a food processor, combine the seeds and nuts and pulse/purée until crumbly (do not over-purée, or the mixture will start to turn to nut butter!).

I use Skeet and Ike's dry roasted pumpkin seeds, which are nice because they have a lot of flavor and you do not need to add any salt. If you use raw pumpkin seeds and/or toast them yourself, add a little salt before puréeing, a few pinches to taste.

Raw green pistachios or hemp seed nuts are great substitutions for the pine nuts.

Roasted Yellow Pepper Sauce

Wheat-Free

This sauce tastes rich and luxurious, and is delicious over Celebrity Adzuki Bean and Rice Cakes (p. 86). Also try it tossed into pasta, or over grains, beans, and other veggie patties. Once you have the peppers roasted, your blender does the rest of the work!

3	**medium-large yellow bell peppers (about 1¼ - 1½ cups once roasted)**
2 tsp	**extra-virgin olive oil (for roasting peppers)**
⅛ tsp	**sea salt (for roasting peppers)**
⅓ cup	**water (see note)**
2 - 2½ tbsp	**extra-virgin olive oil (for sauce)**
1 tbsp	**apple cider vinegar**
1	**small clove garlic**
¾ - 1 tsp	**Dijon mustard**
¾ - 1 tsp	**fresh rosemary, roughly chopped**
½ tsp	**sea salt**
	freshly ground black pepper to taste (optional)

Set oven to broil/grill. Cut peppers into four sections away from their cores, removing seeds and white veins. Place the cut peppers on a baking sheet lined with parchment paper. Rub a little olive oil on the skin sides of the peppers, and sprinkle with sea salt. Place under the broiler and let grill for 12-15 minutes, until the peppers have blistered and blackened in spots. Remove and transfer peppers to a large bowl and immediately cover with a plate or plastic wrap so the peppers will "sweat." Once the peppers are cool enough to handle and the skins have loosened, remove the skins from the peppers and discard. With a handblender or in a blender, combine the peppers (and any juices in the bowl) with the remaining ingredients and purée until very smooth. Adjust to taste with additional sea salt and fresh ground black pepper, if desired. Serve at room temperature, warmed a little, or even chilled!

For a thinner sauce, add a little more water. Alternatively, you can turn this sauce into a dip for pitas, tortilla chips, etc. by adding less water, just several tablespoons.

Roasty Toasty Sunflower Seeds

Wheat-Free

Transform sunflower seeds from ordinary to interesting with this basic recipe. Sprinkle them on salads, soups, or eat straight as a snack!

½ cup	**sunflower seeds**
1½ tsp	**toasted sesame oil**
1½ - 2 tsp	**balsamic vinegar**
few pinches	**sea salt**

Preheat oven to 400°F (204°C). In a bowl, combine all the ingredients together. Transfer to a baking sheet lined with parchment paper and bake for 7-10 minutes, tossing once or twice throughout, until golden and fragrant. Keep a close eye on them, as the seeds can go from golden to burned very quickly!

Instead of the oven, you could use a toaster oven for this small amount. Line the toaster oven tray with parchment paper.

Sesame Mustard Tahini Sauce

Wheat-Free

This is a rich and zesty sauce that's very versatile: it can be tossed into cooked pasta, beans, or steamed veggies; drizzled over cooked grains, fresh salads, or veggie patties (such as Moroccan Chickpea Patties, p. 97); or even mashed into leftover tofu for a snappy sandwich filling. So many possibilities!

½ cup	water (+ 1-2 tbsp or more, adjust to desired consistency) (see note)
½ cup	tahini
⅓ cup	apple cider vinegar
1	small clove garlic, chopped
1½ tbsp	honey alternative (see note)
3 tbsp	tamari
2 tsp	Dijon mustard
2½ - 3 tsp	toasted sesame oil
¼ - ½ tsp	sea salt (adjust to taste)

With a handblender or in a blender, combine all the ingredients, starting with ½ cup of the water. Thin out with extra water to desired consistency, and season to taste with additional sea salt and/or honey alternative, if desired.

You can add extra tablespoons of water to thin this sauce to a consistency you like – the additional water will also dilute the flavors a little if you find a thicker sauce a bit intense. This sauce also thickens after refrigerating, so you may want to stir in another teaspoon or two of water. Keep in mind that a thicker sauce is good for sandwiches, patties, grains, and spring rolls, or to use as a dip, and a thinner sauce is best for tossing with pasta, or to use as a salad dressing.

For the honey alternative, I like using agave nectar in this sauce, but you can use another liquid sweetener of choice.

Simple Cider Vinaigrette

Wheat-Free

Every time I make this recipe, I think "Simple Simon" … all those nursery rhymes! That aside, a vinaigrette cannot get much simpler than this, using very basic pantry items. It has a stronger vinegar flavor than some of my other vinaigrette recipes, and is excellent tossed with a simple salad of mixed greens and cherry tomatoes!

¼ **cup**	**apple cider vinegar**
1 tsp	**Dijon mustard**
½ **tsp**	**sea salt**
	freshly ground black pepper to taste
1½ tbsp	**pure maple syrup (or more to taste)**
¼ **cup + 1 tbsp**	**extra-virgin olive oil (or less/more if desired)**

With a handblender or in a blender, combine all the ingredients except the oil and purée. Continue blending and drizzle in the oil. Season to taste with additional sea salt and freshly ground black pepper, if desired.

Sweet Maple-Hemp Vinaigrette

Wheat-Free

Hemp seed oil is abundant with essential fatty acids, and has a pleasant nutty flavor. This sweet and mellow vinaigrette is one of my favorites, and is one tasty way to include healthy hemp oil in your diet!

⅓ cup	pure maple syrup
¼ cup	apple cider vinegar
2 tsp	tamari
1	small clove garlic, chopped
1½ tsp	Dijon mustard
½ tsp	sea salt
	freshly ground pepper to taste
3½ - 4 tbsp	hemp seed oil
2 tbsp	extra-virgin olive oil (can use more/less, or additional hemp seed oil)

With a handblender or in a blender, combine all the ingredients except the oils and purée. Continue blending and drizzle in the hemp and olive oils. Season to taste with additional sea salt and freshly ground black pepper, if desired.

Salads,

Sides,

Spreads,

& Appetizers

Cannellini Bean Yam Hummus

Wheat-Free

This is a smoky-sweet hummus, a tasty change from the traditional chickpea version. The cannellini beans and yams make the mixture creamy and sweet, while the chipotle sauce and toasted pine nuts add depth and crunch. Keep cannellini beans on hand in the freezer (see Guide to Cooking Beans, p. 165), or use canned.

1½ cups	cooked cannellini beans (see note)
¾ cup	cooked yam (not packed; would be too sweet) (see note)
3 tbsp	freshly squeezed lime or lemon juice, or combination
1	small to medium clove garlic, chopped
2 tbsp	extra-virgin olive oil
¾ - 1 tsp	chipotle hot sauce
½ tsp	sea salt
	freshly ground black pepper to taste
¼ cup	toasted pine nuts (plus extra for garnish) (see Cooking Notes, p. 167)
2 tbsp	fresh cilantro, chopped (garnish) (optional)

In a blender or a food processor, combine all the ingredients except the pine nuts and optional cilantro and purée until very smooth, scraping down the sides of the bowl a few times throughout. Once smooth, add the pine nuts and purée just a little, leaving some texture (you can blend until smooth if you like, but I prefer a bit of texture). Season to taste with extra sea salt, black pepper, and chipotle sauce, if desired. Serve in a bowl drizzled with a little extra-virgin olive oil, and a sprinkling of pine nuts and cilantro.

Makes 5-6 servings or more as an appetizer with bread, chips, and/or veggies.

Instead of cannellini beans, you can use another white bean, or chickpeas. If using chickpeas, add a couple of tablespoons of water or extra olive oil (or combination). Chickpeas are drier than cannellini beans, so the oil and/or water will help make the chickpea version smoother.

To cook the yam, place it whole (unpeeled) on a baking sheet lined with parchment paper. Bake at 400°F (204°C) for 45-60 minutes (depending on size) until very soft when pierced.

As well as a dip for bread and veggies, use this hummus as a spread on bread or in pitas with veggies for a lively sandwich, or on a flour tortilla with veggies for a wrap. Spread on a pizza shell or pre-baked flour tortillas and top as you like for pizzas (see Hummus Tortilla Pizzas, p. 95). Spread on a whole grain, or use in a casserole, such as Vicki's Hummus-Quinoa Casserole (p. 110), replacing the traditional chickpea hummus with this version!

Chipotle Yam Wedges

Wheat-Free

The smoky heat of chipotle sauce contrasts so perfectly with the sweet, soft texture of the yam wedges making these a different, delish side dish!

2 tbsp	**extra-virgin olive oil**
2½ - 3 tsp	**chipotle hot sauce**
2 lbs	**yams, peeled and cut in wedges**
¼ tsp	**sea salt**

Preheat oven to 400°F (204°C). In a bowl, combine the olive oil and the chipotle hot sauce, then add the yam wedges and toss. Transfer to a baking sheet lined with parchment paper (including any remaining oil in the bowl), and season with the sea salt. Bake for 55-65 minutes, tossing once or twice throughout, until the wedges have browned and are soft when pierced. Season to taste with additional sea salt if desired.

Makes 3-4 servings as a side dish.

Creamy Hummus

Wheat-Free

Family and friends have remarked that this delicate hummus is the best they've ever had. It's creamy with a good amount of lemon and just a hint of garlic, unlike some versions that are overpowered by garlic and/or tahini. Try it also on Hummus Tortilla Pizzas (p. 95) and in Vicki's Hummus-Quinoa Casserole (p. 110).

2 cups	cooked chickpeas (garbanzo beans) (canned is okay; see Guide to Cooking Beans, p. 165)
3½ - 5 tbsp	freshly squeezed lemon juice (adjust to taste)
3 tbsp	tahini
2 tbsp	extra-virgin olive oil
1	small or medium clove garlic, sliced
½ tsp	toasted sesame oil
½ tsp	sea salt
¼ cup	water (or less/more as desired)
	freshly ground black pepper to taste

In a blender or a food processor, combine all the ingredients and purée until smooth, adding a little water at first, then more if desired to thin it (for the Hummus Tortilla Pizzas, keep the hummus thick). Scrape down the sides of the bowl several times throughout and purée again until very smooth. Season to taste with additional salt, pepper, and/or lemon juice. Serve in a large bowl, drizzled with extra-virgin olive oil.

Makes 5-6 servings or more as an appetizer with bread, chips, and/or veggies.

Fresh Jicama Salad

Wheat-Free

This salad is super for a large crowd at a picnic, potluck, or a barbecue (veggie burgers, of course!) on a hot summer's day. The jicama is refreshing and offers lots of crunch.

2 - 2½ cups	jicama, coarse skin trimmed and inner flesh julienned (roughly 1 large jicama) (see note)
1½ cups	cucumber, seeds removed and julienned (peeling optional)
1½ cups	red or yellow pepper, julienned
1 cup	carrot, julienned
¼ cup	pumpkin seeds (roasted is best)
3 - 4 tbsp	dried cranberries
1 - 2 tbsp	fresh basil, chopped
1 - 2 tbsp	fresh parsley, coriander, or tarragon, chopped
2½ - 3 tbsp	extra-virgin olive oil
2 tbsp	freshly squeezed lemon juice
¼ tsp	sea salt
	freshly ground pepper to taste

In a large bowl, combine the veggies, pumpkin seeds, cranberries, and fresh herbs. Add the olive oil and toss to coat. Add the lemon juice, salt, and pepper, and toss through to coat. Serve immediately, otherwise the veggies will wilt and soften. Season further to taste as desired.

Makes 6 or more servings as a side dish.

The veggies in this salad are all julienned, which means cut in long, thin, strips. The cup measurements are rough because it is difficult to be exact measuring long strips of vegetables. For the jicama, you will need to trim at least ¼" of the coarse skin to reach the crisp inner flesh. If you have one that is brownish inside, it is not very fresh, although you may be able to salvage some whiter portions. Check the glossary for tips on selecting jicama, and buy two if you are unsure; you can always use the other for another meal! This is a very flexible recipe, so if you want more of one vegetable and less of another – no problem. Just use about the same total amount of veggies.

Kalamata Walnut Tapenade

A twist on the standard olive tapenade, this one combines both black and kalamata olives along with toasted walnuts. The taste is still pungent and flavorful, but not overpowering and overly salty as some olive tapenades can be.

½ cup	pitted kalamata olives (see note)
½ cup	pitted black olives (use canned; drain and rinse) (see note)
½ cup + 2 tbsp	toasted walnuts (see Cooking Notes, p. 167)
¼ cup	fresh parsley, chopped
2 - 3 tbsp	extra-virgin olive oil
1½ - 2 tbsp	freshly squeezed lemon juice
1	small clove garlic
1 - 2 tsp	fresh thyme, chopped
1 tsp	Dijon mustard
	sea salt to taste
	freshly ground black pepper to taste

In a blender or a food processor, combine all the ingredients. Pulse and process until the mixture is mostly uniform, but has a little chunky consistency. Season to taste with additional lemon juice, salt, or pepper.

Makes 5-6 servings or more with bread, pitas, etc.

Save yourself the time and work of pitting your own olives and buy pitted kalamata olives in the deli section of your grocery store.

In addition to serving this tapenade with bread, pitas, crackers, or veggies, this recipe makes a wonderful spread for sandwiches. Also try spreading some on a pizza crust before adding other toppings – amazing flavor for your pie!

Lemon-Herb Tofu

Wheat-Free

The lemon juice and tamari bake into the tofu, and the dried herbs and oil coat each savory piece. If you don't like to fuss with tofu but want incredible flavor, this recipe is a must!

3½ - 4 tbsp	**freshly squeezed lemon juice**
2 tbsp	**tamari**
2- 2½ tbsp	**extra-virgin olive oil**
1½ tsp	**dried oregano**
1 tsp	**dried thyme**
½ tsp	**dried basil**
½ tsp	**honey alternative**
few pinches	**freshly ground black pepper**
1 350-g pkg	**(12-oz) extra-firm tofu, cut into squares about ¼" - ½" thick, and patted gently to remove excess moisture**

Preheat oven to 375°F (190°C). In an 8"x12" baking dish, combine the lemon juice, tamari, olive oil, oregano, thyme, basil, honey alternative, and pepper, and stir through until well incorporated. Add the tofu and coat each side. Bake covered for 15 minutes. Turn the tofu over, and continue to bake uncovered for another 13-15 minutes, turning again when there are just a few minutes of cooking time remaining. At this time, the tofu should have soaked up most of the marinade. Remove from oven and let cool a little before serving; pour any remaining herbs and oil over the tofu.

Makes 4 - 6 sevings as a side dish.

This tofu makes a very tasty sandwich filling. Take any leftovers and mash, or pulse in a food processor until crumbly, then mix with vegan mayonnaise.

Lemon Rosemary Potatoes

These are potatoes with personality! The lemon juice soaks right into the taters, and the fresh rosemary and olive oil are perfect potato partners. A tempting side dish for just about any entrée!

2½ - 3 lbs	(1 - 1⅓ kg) Yukon Gold or red potatoes, cut in chunks (roughly 1 - 1½")
3 - 3½ tbsp	extra-virgin olive oil
2½ - 3 tbsp	freshly squeezed lemon juice
2 - 3 tsp	fresh rosemary, chopped
½ tsp	sea salt
	freshly ground black pepper to taste

Preheat oven to 400°F (204°C). In a large bowl, toss the potatoes with the olive oil, roughly ½ of the lemon juice, and the rosemary, salt, and pepper. Transfer the potatoes to a deep-rimmed baking pan lined with two sheets of parchment paper. Bake for 45-50 minutes. Sprinkle with the remaining lemon juice, then bake for another 10-15 minutes, or until the potatoes are golden brown and tender. Season to taste with additional sea salt and pepper if desired.

Makes 4 servings as a side dish.

Mellow Millet-Quinoa Pilaf

Wheat-Free

This delicate pilaf pairs a stickier grain, millet, with the lighter, more easily separable quinoa. Try serving with a bean dish such as Roasted Pepper Cannellini Bean Sauce (p. 100), with a stirfry, or as a base for soups or stews.

½ cup	millet
½ cup	quinoa
1 tbsp	extra-virgin olive oil
2	shallots or 1 small red onion, diced
½ tsp	sea salt
2⅓ cups	water
¼ cup	hemp seed nuts (optional) (see note)

Rinse the millet and quinoa and let drain. In a saucepan over medium heat, combine the quinoa and millet and cook for 5-7 minutes, stirring occasionally. Once the grains are dry and there is a nutty aroma, reduce heat to low. Add the olive oil, shallots or onion, and sea salt, cover and let cook for a couple of minutes, stirring once or twice. Add the water, increase heat to medium high and bring to a boil, then reduce heat to simmer and cover. Let cook for 17-20 minutes, then remove from heat and let sit covered for 4-5 minutes.

Fluff grains through with a fork. If water is not all absorbed, let sit for another few minutes, or return to a low heat for a couple of minutes. Just before serving, stir in the optional hemp seed nuts (or any other ingredients, see note), season to taste with additional sea salt if desired, and serve. Drizzle on extra olive oil if desired, or Balsamic-Garlic Flax Oil (p. 44).

Makes 4 servings as a side dish.

If desired, you can add extra seasonings to this dish. For instance, when cooking the shallots or onion, add some curry powder and mustard seeds, or some cumin, cinnamon, and coriander. Or once the pilaf is cooked, toss in some fresh herbs like finely chopped oregano, mint, or coriander!

The hemp seed nuts add texture and additional nutritional value to this dish. You could substitute (or add) roasted pumpkin seeds, green pistachios, and/or some dried cranberries for a twist!

Miso-Curry Roasted Potatoes

Wheat-Free

A spiced-up spud makeover! Try serving with Molasses Baked Beans (p. 96) or a salad topped with Creamy Orange-Poppy Seed Dressing (p. 47).

2½ - 3 lbs	(1 - 1⅓ kg) Yukon Gold or red potatoes, cut in small chunks (or nugget potatoes, simply cut in half or thirds)
3 - 3½ tbsp	olive oil
⅛ tsp	sea salt
few pinches	freshly ground black pepper
1 tbsp	mild miso (e.g., barley or brown rice miso)
½ tbsp	water
1 - 1½ tsp	mild curry paste
½ tbsp	olive oil (for the paste)

Preheat oven to 400°F (204°C). In a large bowl, toss the potatoes with the oil, salt, and pepper, then transfer to a baking sheet lined with parchment paper. In another bowl, mix the miso with the water and curry powder until well combined, then stir in the olive oil and set aside (do not add to the potatoes yet). Roast the potatoes for roughly 45-55 minutes, tossing once or twice throughout, until the potatoes are nearly cooked – just tender and lightly browned. Remove from oven and coat with the miso paste. Return and roast for another 5 minutes, until the potatoes are nicely browned. Season to taste with additional sea salt and pepper if desired.

Makes 4 servings as a side dish.

Pan-Fried Eggplant

Eggplant is not everyone's favorite vegetable; it can have a rubbery texture and a bland or bitter taste. But when prepared and seasoned properly, it's delicious. Here, pre-salted eggplant rounds are double-dipped in seasoned breadcrumbs and fried until golden; the crunchy coating envelopes the tender eggplant, which melts in your mouth. These are best hot from the pan, so make as a side dish for 4-5 or as a nibbler for a larger crowd.

1	medium-large eggplant, sliced in rounds about ½" thick
¾ - 1 tsp	sea salt (for eggplants)
1 cup	good quality breadcrumbs (see note)
½ cup	unbleached all-purpose flour (see note)
½ tsp	sea salt (for breadcrumb coating)
1 tsp	dried oregano
1 tsp	paprika
¼ tsp	chili powder
	freshly ground black pepper to taste
⅓ cup	plain non-dairy milk
¼ - ⅓ cup	olive oil (or more as needed for 2 batches of frying)

Place the sliced eggplant in a colander and sprinkle with the sea salt. Toss gently, then let sit for about 30 minutes. (The salt will help extrude the eggplant's bitter juices and keep it from absorbing extra oil when frying.) Rinse the eggplant well with cold water and pat dry. In a large bowl, combine the breadcrumbs, flour, salt, spices, and pepper. Take about ⅓ of the mixture and place it in another bowl. Pour the non-dairy milk in a separate bowl. To coat the eggplant, first dip each slice into the bowl with the ⅓ breadcrumb mixture (pat gently to stick), then into the milk, and then into the other bowl of breadcrumb mixture (again, pat gently to stick). Repeat until finished.

In a skillet over high/medium-high heat, add roughly ½ of the olive oil. Once oil is hot, working in batches, carefully add the eggplant slices and fry 5-7 minutes on each side until golden brown and crispy (adjust heat as needed). Serve as is or with a warm tomato sauce or other dipping/drizzling sauce.

Makes 4 - 5 servings as a side dish.

For a wheat-free version, use spelt flour and make your own breadcrumbs using a wheat-free bread.

Pecan Fried Wild Rice

Wheat-Free

This dish is simple and very flavorful. It's also surprisingly fast to prepare, and you'll save even more time by cooking the rice a day or two in advance.

1½ tbsp	extra-virgin olive oil
4 - 4½ cups	cooked wild rice/brown rice mixture (see note)
	freshly ground black pepper to taste
½ cup	frozen green peas
¾ cup	green onions, chopped (roughly 1 bunch; use the green portion and some of the light-green portion)
½ cup	toasted pecans, broken or chopped (see Cooking Notes, p. 167)
2 tbsp	tamari
1 tsp	toasted sesame oil

In a skillet over medium heat, add the oil. When the oil is hot, add the cooked rice, season with pepper, and sauté for 2-3 minutes, stirring occasionally. Add the frozen peas and stir through for another 2-3 minutes, then add the green onions, pecans, and tamari. Stir until the peas are heated through and the green onions have wilted and cooked a little, about 3-4 minutes. Turn off the heat, stir in the toasted sesame oil, and season to taste with sea salt and pepper if desired.

Makes 4-5 servings as a side dish.

You can use all wild or brown rice, or a wild and basmati rice mix. Wild rice is particularly nice to use because it adds an earthy flavor that works well with the other ingredients. I typically use roughly ¾ cup each of wild rice and brown rice. Rinse the rice, and combine with close to 4 cups of water and a few pinches of sea salt in a saucepan. Bring to a boil, stir through, then reduce heat to low and cover. Let simmer for 45-50 minutes until the water is absorbed and the wild rice is tender and has opened up. Let cool a little, or refrigerate until ready to use. If you use more wild rice, you will need more water; see Guide To Cooking Grains, p. 164.

Quinoa Spring Salad

Wheat-Free

My mother was visiting from Newfoundland when I was testing this recipe. She was thrilled to be my "taste tester," and this dish became one of her favorites! It's a breeze to make, especially if you cook the quinoa in advance, and it has fabulous flavors and textures. Mom returned home with this recipe in hand, along with my scribbles on how to pronounce "quinoa" (remember, "keen-wa," Mom!).

½ cup	frozen green peas (plus 2 cups boiling water to soak peas)
3 cups	cooked quinoa, cooled (see Guide To Cooking Grains, p. 164)
¾ - 1 cup	roasted red bell peppers, chopped (roughly 2 medium or 1½ large peppers), or raw red bell peppers, finely chopped
¼ cup	green onions, thinly sliced
⅓ - ½ cup	cucumber, seeds removed and diced (peeling optional)
⅓ cup	green pistachios or toasted pine nuts (see Cooking Notes, p. 167), or combination
¼ cup	hemp seed nuts (or more, if desired)
2 - 4 tbsp	cilantro, parsley, or basil, chopped
¼ tsp	sea salt
3½ - 4 tbsp	Simple Cider Vinaigrette, p. 57 (or more, if desired) (see note)

In a bowl, soak the frozen peas in the boiling water. Let sit until the peas have warmed through. Drain peas and pat dry. In a large bowl, combine the peas with the remaining ingredients. Toss through to mix well. Serve immediately or refrigerate in an airtight container.

Makes 5-6 servings as a side dish.

This vinaigrette works well with this salad because it's not overly complicated with too many flavors, and has a good amount of vinegar that works well here. You can use another vinaigrette of choice if you like, however, or even some olive oil and lemon juice, along with a little extra sea salt.

Sage Roasted Taro Root and Sweet Potato

Wheat-Free

Instead of the usual potatoes, pick up some taro root, sweet potato (or yam), and fresh sage and try out these tempting taters!

1 - 1½ lb	(½ - ⅓ kg) taro root, peeled and cut into small chunks, roughly 1" - 1½" thick (see note)
1 - 1½ lb	(½ - ⅓ kg) sweet potatoes, peeled and cut into small chunks, roughly 1" - 1½" thick (see note)
2½ - 3 tbsp	extra-virgin olive oil
1½ - 2 tsp	fresh sage, minced
½ tsp	sea salt
⅛ - ¼ tsp	freshly grated nutmeg (optional)
	freshly ground black pepper to taste

Preheat oven to 400°F (204°C). In a bowl, toss the taro root and sweet potatoes with the oil, sage, salt, nutmeg, and pepper, then transfer to a baking sheet lined with parchment paper. Bake for 50-60 minutes, tossing once or twice throughout, until lightly browned and tender. Season to taste with additional sea salt and pepper if desired.

Makes 3-4 servings as a side dish.

You can use an assortment of different roots and tubers in this recipe to replace some or all of the taro or sweet potato. A combination of yams, parsnips, and a little white potato is delicious; you could also try some rutabega, celeriac, or even beets!

Soups

& Stews

Chipotle Corn Black Bean Soup

Wheat-Free

Enjoy this smoky, spicy soup with some whole-grain bread and a salad dressed with Citrus Mint Vinaigrette (p. 45).

1½ - 2 tbsp	olive oil		3½ cups	cooked black beans (or roughly 2 14-oz cans)
1 - 1½ cup	onion, chopped		2 cups	vegetable stock
3	medium to large cloves garlic, chopped		1½ - 2 cups	water
½ tsp	sea salt		2 tbsp	balsamic vinegar
	freshly ground black pepper to taste		2 tsp	tamari
1½ cups	celery, chopped		½ - 1 tsp	chipotle hot sauce (or more, to taste)
1½ cups	carrots, chopped		2	bay leaves
4 tsp	ground cumin		1½ cups	frozen corn kernels
1 tsp	mustard seeds		4 - 5	fresh lime wedges (to finish)
1 tsp	ground coriander		1	avocado, sliced (garnish)
¼ tsp	ground cardamon			
¼ - ⅓ cups	sun-dried tomatoes, chopped			

In a large pot over medium heat, heat the oil. Add the onions, garlic, sea salt, and black pepper. Stir through, cover, and let cook for a few minutes. Add the celery, carrots, spices, and sun-dried tomatoes, stir again, cover, and let cook for another 5-7 minutes, until the veggies start to soften. Add the beans, stock, 1½ cups of the water (reserve ½ cup), balsamic vinegar, tamari, hot sauce, and bay leaves. Increase heat to bring to a boil, then reduce heat to medium-low and let simmer for 15-20 minutes. Remove bay leaves, and using a handblender, purée the soup until it is somewhat smooth but still has some texture. Stir in the corn. If you want to thin out the soup, add the remaining ½ cup of water, or more. Cover and let the soup simmer for another few minutes. Season to taste with additional sea salt, black pepper, and chipotle hot sauce, if desired. Serve with a few squeezes of lime juice (a must with this soup!) and garnish with avocado slices.

Makes 6 or more servings.

Earthy Lentil Soup

Wheat-Free

A savory, comforting soup that's easy to make. Freeze a couple of portions and pull out on those nights when only a warm bowl of soup and crusty bread will do!

1½ - 2 tbsp	olive oil
1¼ - 1½ cups	red onion, diced
1½ cups	celery, diced
1 cup	carrot, diced
4	medium-large cloves garlic, minced
½ tsp	sea salt
	freshly ground black pepper to taste
1 tsp	dried oregano
1 tsp	dried savory
½ tsp	dried rosemary
½ tsp	dried thyme
½ tsp	curry powder
2 cups	brown lentils, rinsed
2 cups	vegetable stock
6 - 7 cups	water
1 - 1½ tbsp	tamari
2½ - 3 tsp	blackstrap molasses
2 - 3	bay leaves
¼ cup	fresh parsley, chopped
1 - 1½ tbsp	freshly squeezed lemon juice
1 - 2 tbsp	fresh thyme, finely chopped (optional)
	lemon wedges (to finish)

In a large pot over medium heat, heat the oil. Add the onion, celery, carrot, garlic, salt, pepper, dried herbs and curry powder. Stir through, cover, and cook for a couple of minutes, stirring occasionally. Add the lentils, vegetable stock, water, tamari, molasses, bay leaves and stir through. Increase heat to bring to a boil, then reduce heat to medium-low, cover and let cook for 55-60 minutes, until the lentils are very soft and soup has thickened. Just before serving, stir in the parsley, lemon juice, and thyme. If you want to thin out the soup, add more water as desired. Season to taste with additional sea salt and pepper. Serve with a few squeezes of fresh lemon juice.

Makes 6 or more servings.

Kamut Bean Stew

This is a delightful, easy stew with interesting flavors and textures. The whole kamut grain is a little chewy when cooked, and contrasts well with the vegetables and soft beans. This has become one of my favorite comfort soups!

1½ tbsp	olive oil
2½ cups	red onion, chopped
2 cups	celery root (celeriac), chopped
1 cup	celery, chopped
¾ - 1 tsp	sea salt (adjust to taste)
	freshly ground black pepper to taste
1 tbsp	fennel seeds
1 - 2 tsp	coriander seeds
¾ tsp	dill seeds
1 tsp	dry mustard
¾ cup	whole kamut grain (kamut berries) (see note)
1 28-oz can	(796-ml) diced tomatoes
2 cups	vegetable stock
2 cups	water
2	bay leaves
2 15-oz cans	(398-ml) kidney beans (rinsed and drained)
1½ - 2 cups	cooked adzuki beans (or other small bean)

In a large pot over medium heat, heat the olive oil. Add the onion, celery root, celery, salt, pepper, fennel seeds, coriander seeds, dill seeds, dry mustard, and kamut. Stir through, cover, and let cook for 5-7 minutes, stirring occasionally; reduce heat if the onions are sticking. Once onions have softened, add the tomatoes, vegetable stock, water and bay leaves. Stir through and increase heat to bring to a boil. Reduce heat to low, cover and simmer for about 50 minutes. Add the beans, stir through, cover, and let cook for another 15-20 minutes or longer, until the kamut is soft and chewy. Season to taste with additional salt and pepper.

Makes 7-8 servings.

You can use other grains instead of kamut and adjust cooking time accordingly; for instance, the cooking time for whole spelt, wheatberries, or wild rice will be 10-20 minutes less; and if you use brown or brown basmati rice, the cooking time will be reduced by about a ½ hour. Refer to the Guide To Cooking Grains (p. 164) for more information.

Last-Minute Chili & Taco Filling

Throw together canned kidney beans, diced tomatoes, chili sauce, and some veggie ground, plus a few other ingredients, and you'll get this robust chili that doubles as a taco filling (see note).

1½ - 2 tbsp	olive oil
1	large red onion, finely chopped (roughly 3 cups) (see note)
3 - 4	medium-large cloves garlic, minced (see note)
¾ - 1 tsp	sea salt
	freshly ground black pepper to taste
2 tsp	chili powder
1 tsp	paprika
1 tsp	dried oregano
1 cup	green bell pepper (or combination of green and red bell pepper), diced
1 28-oz can	(796-ml) diced tomatoes
½ cup	chili sauce
2 15-oz cans	(398-ml) kidney beans (rinsed and drained)
1 12-oz pkg	(340-g) (or similar) veggie ground round (Italian or Mexican flavors are good)
	chipotle hot sauce or other hot sauce to taste (optional)

In a large pot over medium heat, heat the oil. Add the onions, garlic, salt, pepper, chili powder, paprika, and oregano. Cover and let cook for 6-8 minutes, stirring occasionally; reduce heat if the onions are sticking. When the onions have softened, add the remaining ingredients, stir through, and increase heat to high to bring to a boil. Reduce heat to low, cover, and let simmer for 20-25 minutes, stirring occasionally. For a thinner consistency, add more water as desired. Season to taste with additional salt, pepper, or hot sauce.

Makes 5-6 servings.

Use this chili for super tacos! Bake taco shells for a few minutes until just golden and crispy. Fill shells with chili and top with grated non-dairy cheese, shredded lettuce, and guacamole, which you can make by mashing a couple of avocados (leave some texture) with a few squeezes of lemon or lime juice, a few pinches of sea salt, and some chopped fresh coriander. Totally delicious!

Save chopping time by tossing the onion (cut in large chunks) and garlic in a food processor, and pulsing through until minced.

Roasted Tomato Bean Stew

This simple stew boasts great flavor from the smoky tomatoes and seasonings, and is thick and hearty from the rice and beans. My daughter's "soup of choice"!

1 - 1½ tbsp	olive oil	2 28-oz cans	(796-ml) Muir Glen Fire Roasted Diced Tomatoes (see note)
1 cup	celery, diced		
1 cup	red onion, diced		
4 - 5	large cloves garlic, minced	⅓ cup	wild rice (uncooked), rinsed
1 tsp	sea salt	⅓ cup	brown rice, rinsed (short grain is good)
	freshly ground black pepper to taste	2 - 2½ cups	water
2 tsp	dried oregano	2 - 3	bay leaves
1 tsp	dried rosemary	½ - ¾ tsp	honey alternative
⅛ tsp	dried ground sage	2½ - 3 cups	cooked adzuki beans (or other small bean)
2½ - 3 tsp	vegetarian Worcestershire sauce		chipotle hot sauce to taste (optional)
1 tbsp	hoisin sauce		

In a large pot over medium heat, heat the oil. Add the celery, onion, garlic, salt, pepper (fairly generous is good), and dried herbs. Stir through, cover, and let cook for a few minutes. Add the Worcestershire and hoisin sauces, tomatoes, wild and brown rice, 2 cups of the water, bay leaves, and honey alternative. Stir through, and increase heat to high to bring to a boil. Reduce heat to low, cover, and let simmer for about 45 minutes. Add the beans, stir through, cover, and let simmer for another 10-15 minutes, until both the brown and wild rice are cooked through and the wild rice has opened up some. The stew will be quite thick, so if desired, add the remaining ½ cup of water, or more. Remove bay leaves, and season to taste with additional sea salt and pepper.

Makes 6-8 servings.

If you can't find Muir Glen Fire Roasted Tomatoes, use regular diced tomatoes and simply season more with a little extra vegan Worcestershire sauce, a few dashes of chipotle hot sauce (for that roasted smoky flavor), and a dash of liquid smoke if you like.

Three-Bean Curry Tomato Soup

Wheat-Free

This soup is a must for curry enthusiasts! It's straight-forward to make, and combines three kinds of healthful beans with vivid curry seasonings (without too much heat!). Serve with a cooked grain or some whole-grain bread for a complete meal.

1½ - 2 tbsp	olive oil
2 cups	celery, finely chopped
1½ - 2 cups	onion, finely chopped
1 cup	carrot, finely chopped
¼ tsp	sea salt
	freshly ground black pepper to taste
1 tbsp	mustard seeds
1½ - 2 tbsp	mild curry paste (or more for additional heat)
½ tsp	ground ginger
1 tsp	ground fennel
½ tsp	ground cardamom
¼ tsp	cinnamon
1 28-oz can	(796-ml) diced tomatoes
2 cups	cooked chickpeas (garbanzo beans) (see note)
2 cups	cooked black beans (see note)
1 cup	dry red lentils
2 cups	vegetable stock
3 - 3½ cups	water
2	bay leaves
1 tsp	honey alternative

In a large pot over medium heat, heat the oil. Add the celery, onion, carrot, salt, and pepper, and stir through. Add the mustard seeds, curry paste, ginger, fennel, cardamom, and cinnamon. Stir through, cover, and let cook for 6-8 minutes. Add the remaining ingredients. Stir through and increase heat to high to bring to a boil. Reduce heat to low, cover, and let simmer for 15-20 minutes. For a thinner consistency, add a little extra water. Remove bay leaves, and season to taste with additional sea salt and black pepper.

Makes 8 or more servings.

The chickpeas and black beans add contrasting textures and colors, but you can substitute cooked adzuki beans, cannellini beans, pinto beans, kidney beans ... whatever you have on hand!

Winter Harvest Soup

Wheat-Free

This savory soup is hearty yet mellow, perfect for those who don't like spicy soups, and anyone wanting some belly-warming comfort food to chase away those winter chills!

2 tbsp	olive oil
1¾ - 2 cups	red onion, chopped
2 cups	rutabega, chopped in small chunks
¼ - ½ tsp	sea salt
	freshly ground black pepper to taste
1½ cups	celery, chopped
2½ - 3 cups	yam, chopped in small chunks (see note)
2½ cups	sweet potato, chopped in small chunks (see note)
2 tsp	dried oregano
1 tsp	dried thyme
1 tsp	dried savory
1 tsp	dried rosemary
2 tsp	dried mustard
3½ cups	vegetable stock
3 cups	water
2	large dried bay leaves
3½ - 4 cups	cooked beans, any kind (I use adzuki beans and black-eyed peas)
5 - 7 cups	baby bok choy, chopped (if using regular bok choy, use leafy portion)
1 tsp	molasses
1 - 2 tbsp	fresh oregano or thyme, chopped (see note)
2 - 3 tbsp	arrowroot powder, dissolved in several tbsp water (optional)

You can mix the quantities of sweet potatoes and yams to get 5 - 5½ cups total.

While the fresh herbs are lovely here, if you don't have them you can increase the amount of dried oregano or thyme by ½ - 1 tsp.

In a large pot over medium heat, heat the oil. Add the onion, rutabega, salt, and pepper. Stir through, cover, and let cook for a few minutes. Add the celery, yams, sweet potatoes, dried herbs and mustard. Stir through, cover, and cook for another 7-8 minutes. Add the stock, water, and bay leaves. Stir through and increase heat to high to bring to a boil. Reduce heat, cover, and let simmer for 14-18 minutes, until the vegetables are tender. Add the beans, bok choy, molasses, and optional fresh herbs. Stir through and cook for just a few minutes, until the bok choy has wilted. For a thicker soup, stir in the arrowroot/water mixture, and while stirring, bring the soup back to a boil just for a minute until it thickens. Remove bay leaves, and season to taste with extra sea salt and a generous amount of ground black pepper (this soup is really good with plenty of pepper).

Makes 8-10 servings.

Main Courses

Broccoli-Mushroom-Walnut Phyllo Pie (or Pasta)

Wheat-Free Option

When testing this recipe, I tried the mixture tossed with pasta, and then, with a few changes as a filling for a phyllo pie. I couldn't choose which to include, so here are both options! The pasta sauce is certainly quicker, but the pie is great for a special occasion.

1 tbsp	olive oil
1 cup	red onion, diced
¼ tsp	sea salt
⅛ tsp	freshly ground black pepper
1 tsp	dried oregano
¼ tsp	dried mustard
2 - 2½ cups	broccoli, roughly chopped
2 - 2½ cups	button mushrooms, chopped
2	medium to large cloves garlic, chopped
2 - 2½ tbsp	tamari
2 - 3 tbsp	plain non-dairy milk
1 tbsp	apple cider vinegar
¼ tsp	freshly ground nutmeg
½ cup	good quality breadcrumbs (see note)
1 cup	toasted walnuts (see Cooking Notes, p. 167)
10 - 12	full sheets phyllo pastry (see note)
2 - 3 tbsp	olive oil (or more/less as needed to brush the phyllo)

In a skillet over medium heat, heat the oil. Add the onions, salt, pepper, oregano, and mustard. Cover and let cook for 4-5 minutes, stirring occasionally. Add broccoli, mushrooms, garlic, and tamari, and cook for another 5 minutes, covered for half the time and then uncovered for the rest, stirring occasionally, until broccoli is bright green and just tender. Remove from heat. In a food processor, combine the sautéed vegetables, milk, vinegar, nutmeg, and breadcrumbs and pulse through until vegetables are somewhat fine but still have some texture. Add the walnuts and pulse until just mixed in; again, you want to incorporate them but keep some texture.

For a wheat-free version, use spelt phyllo pastry and make your own breadcrumbs using wheat-free bread.

To prepare the pie: Preheat oven to 350°F (176°C) and lightly oil an 8"x12" or similar baking dish. Take full sheets of the phyllo and cut them in half along the longest side so that the half sheets will fit the baking dish (cut phyllo according to the size of your dish; you may need more than 12 sheets depending on size). Brush a half sheet of phyllo with a little of the 3 tbsp olive oil, then layer with another sheet and brush again. Repeat until there are 5 layered sheets (you do not need to brush the 5th sheet, as this will have the filling placed on it). Place them in the baking dish and cover with about ⅓ of the filling. Prepare another layer of 5 half sheets, then layer with another ⅓ of filling, then another layer of sheets, and finally the last ⅓ of the filling. Place another half sheet of phyllo on top of the last layer of filling.

To "top" the dish, brush 5 or 6 more half sheets of phyllo with oil. Then, rather than placing them flat, gently bunch each sheet with your fingertips to create loose gathers. Place each bunched sheet on top of the dish, filling the entire surface area. (Don't worry about it looking perfect, as the gathered sheets will look beautiful once baked.) Bake for 27-30 minutes until golden brown. (If refrigerating the dish, bake for a bit longer.) Serve with a drizzle of Lemon Zinger Vinaigrette (p. 51) (a crunchy green salad tossed with this vinaigrette is great on the side), or a little Balsamic-Garlic Flax Oil (p. 44).

Makes 5 or 6 servings, depending on accompaniments.

Pasta Option:

Follow directions for pie with the following changes:
- use only ¼ cup breadcrumbs and omit phyllo pastry
- puréed vegetable mixture should be chunkier
- use an extra 1 cup or more of non-dairy milk
- instead of 3 tbsp olive oil to brush pastry, use 2 tbsp to purée with sauce
- add ¼ - ½ cup of non-dairy parmesan to purée with sauce if desired

Cook the pasta (about ¾ of a 1-lb (450-g) package, rice or kamut for wheat-free version) and reserve ¼ cup of the pasta cooking water. Prepare the sauce in the food processor, then add to the drained pasta with the reserved cooking water and toss well. Add more non-dairy milk if desired. Serve drizzled with extra olive oil and a few squeezes of fresh lemon juice.

Pasta option makes 4 or more servings.

Brown Rice Pizza

Wheat-Free Option

I love to make this true "whole-grain" pizza with some roasted veggies from a nearby deli. But you can roast your own, as described, or use other toppings!

3 cups	water
few pinches	sea salt
1½ cups	brown rice (see note)
2	medium zucchini, sliced lengthwise, then thinly sliced (about 3½ cups)
1	medium red bell pepper, cored and thinly sliced (about 1 cup)
1½ - 2 tbsp	olive oil (for vegetables)
2 tsp	balsamic vinegar
⅛ tsp	sea salt (for vegetables)
½ - 1 tbsp	olive oil (for rice mixture)
2 tsp	dried oregano (or 1 - 2 tbsp fresh oregano, chopped)
2 tsp	dried basil
½ tsp	dried marjoram (or more oregano)
¼ tsp	sea salt (for rice mixture)
few pinches	freshly ground black pepper to taste
¾ - 1 cup	good quality pasta sauce
1 - 1½ tbsp	hoisin sauce (optional)
¼ cup	kalamata or black olives, sliced, or 2 - 3 tbsp capers, rinsed and drained
¼ - ½ cup	mozzarella-style VeganRella cheese, grated (optional)

Rinse rice and combine with water and salt in a saucepan over high heat. Bring to a boil, then reduce heat to low, cover, and let simmer for 45-50 minutes. Preheat oven to 450°F (232°C). In a large bowl, combine the zucchini, red pepper, olive oil, balsamic vinegar, and sea salt, and transfer to a baking sheet lined with parchment paper. Bake for 17-20 minutes, tossing once about halfway through, until golden brown in spots. Remove from oven. Once rice is cooked, transfer to a large bowl and mix in the olive oil, herbs, sea salt, and black pepper (it's easier to mix while warm).

Short-grain brown rice works well because it's sticky, but a longer grain can also be used. Other whole grains can be partially substituted; I've made this recipe with ¾ cup short-grain brown rice, ½ cup millet, and ¼ cup quinoa. If using different grains, adjust the amount of cooking water accordingly (an extra ¼ cup was needed

Preheat oven to 375°F (190°C). On a lightly oiled pizza pan, spread out the rice mixture and press it into the pan until it's sticking together and formed on the pan and up the rim like pizza dough. (To keep your fingers from sticking to the rice, use a small piece of parchment paper to press it down.) Bake rice "shell" for 8-10 minutes. Remove from oven. In a bowl, lightly combine the hoisin sauce and pasta sauce. Spread sauce over the rice shell, especially around outer edge and up the rim. Distribute roasted veggies and olives or capers over top and optional grated VeganRella. Bake for 15-20 minutes. Let cool for a couple of minutes before serving. To serve, use a spatula to divide into wedges and drizzle with Balsamic-Garlic Flax Oil (p. 44).

Makes 4-6 servings.

for the millet combo) and be sure to include a stickier kind, like millet or short-grain brown rice.

For a wheat-free version, omit the hoisin sauce.

Celebrity Adzuki Bean and Rice Cakes

Wheat-Free

A friend of mine was recently cast in a reality TV show. He loves these cakes, and for good reason – they are comforting with a melt-in-your mouth appeal. I decided to give them "celebrity status" just for you, Jim!

1 - 1½ tbsp	olive oil
1½ cups	red onion, chopped
1 cup	celery, chopped
3	medium-large cloves garlic, finely chopped
¼ tsp	sea salt
	freshly ground black pepper to taste
2 cups	cooked brown rice
1½ cups	cooked adzuki or black beans (or another small tender bean)
2½ tbsp	ketchup
2 tbsp	good quality BBQ sauce (check for wheat-free ingredients)
1½ tsp	Dijon mustard
1 - 1½ tsp	fresh rosemary, finely chopped
¾ tsp	sea salt
1½ cups	good quality breadcrumbs
2 tbsp	olive oil (for frying)

In a skillet over medium heat, heat the oil. Add the onion, celery, garlic, sea salt, and pepper. Cook for 6-8 minutes, stirring occasionally, until onions and celery start to soften. In a food processor, combine the onion mixture with the remaining ingredients (except the breadcrumbs and frying oil) and purée gently, pulsing to combine but leaving some texture. Add the breadcrumbs and pulse again a couple of times to combine. Transfer mixture to a bowl, and stir through to fully work in breadcrumbs. Refrigerate for at least ½ hour (chilling will make it firmer and easier to form). Take scoops of the mixture and form into patties with your hands.

In a skillet over medium heat, heat the oil. Add the patties in batches, and fry for 6-9 minutes on each side, until golden and a crust has developed; flip them over only once or twice (the second side will cook quicker than the first). Serve on their own topped with Roasted Yellow Pepper Sauce (p. 54) or other sauce of choice.

Makes 10-11 cakes.

Chickpea Ratatouille

Wheat-Free

This recipe is probably my personal favorite (outside of desserts, of course)! It's much like a ratatouille, but using chickpeas instead of the traditional eggplant and zucchini, and an original spice combination. The result is a dish with a complexity of flavors and the bonus of minimal preparation!

3 cups	cooked chickpeas (garbanzo beans)
1¾ - 2 cups	red onion, finely chopped
3 - 4	medium-large cloves garlic, minced
1 28-oz can	(796-ml) diced tomatoes (see note)
½ cup	red or orange bell pepper, diced
2 tbsp	apple cider vinegar
2 tbsp	olive oil
1 tbsp	freshly grated ginger
2 tsp	honey alternative
2 tsp	mustard seeds
2 tsp	dried basil
1 tsp	dried oregano
½ tsp	dried rosemary
1 tsp	sea salt
⅛ tsp	allspice
	freshly ground black pepper to taste
2	dried bay leaves

Preheat oven to 400°F (204°C). In a large, deep casserole dish, combine all the ingredients except the bay leaves. Stir through until well combined, then embed the bay leaves in the mixture. Cover and bake for 30 minutes. Stir through, cover, and bake for another 35-45 minutes, until the onions are tender and translucent (stir through again once or twice through baking). Remove bay leaves and serve with a cooked grain such as quinoa, wild rice, or brown rice.

Makes 4-5 servings or more, depending on accompaniments.

You can use regular diced tomatoes (Italian flavored ones are good), or Muir Glen Fire Roasted Tomatoes.

Try making burritos with any leftovers! Spoon the mixture onto flour tortillas; roll up and place side-by-side in a baking dish. Sprinkle with some non-dairy cheese and bake! (See directions in Chipotle Veggie-Bean Burritos, p. 90, for more details on burrito-making.)

Chinatown-Style Veggie Spring Rolls

Wheat-Free

These vegan spring rolls are baked instead of fried, and full of flavor with shitake mushrooms, carrots, ginger, and other lively ingredients. They take a little more time than other recipes here, but are fun and unique, and make super party appetizers!

1 22-g pkg	dried sliced shitake mushrooms (roughly 1¾ - 2 cups dried)
3 - 4 cups	boiled water (to soak mushrooms)
1 tbsp	toasted sesame oil
2 tsp	vegan Worcestershire sauce
1½ - 1¾ cups	rice vermicelli noodles, softened (see note)
1 cup	carrots, minced
½ cup	celery, minced
1½ - 2 tbsp	fresh ginger, grated (use 2 tbsp for more heat)
2	small-medium cloves garlic, grated or minced
1 cup	green onions, sliced (mostly green portion)
¼ - ⅓ cup	fresh parsley or coriander, chopped
2½ - 3 tbsp	hoisin sauce
⅛ tsp	Chinese five spice powder (optional)
¼ tsp	sea salt
	freshly ground black pepper to taste
1 1-lb pkg	egg-free egg-roll wrappers (large square size, 7½" x 7½") (see note)
2 - 3 tsp	toasted sesame oil (or more or less, as needed) (to brush spring rolls)
1 - 2 tbsp	toasted sesame seeds (see Cooking Notes, p. 167)

In a large bowl, add the mushrooms and cover with the boiled water. Let soak for several minutes. Drain the mushrooms using a sieve, and press out as much liquid as possible using your hands and/or paper towels. In a bowl, toss the mushrooms with the toasted sesame oil and vegan Worcestershire sauce, and stir through until well mixed and the mushrooms have absorbed the liquid. Roughly chop the softened noodles. In a large bowl, combine the noodles with the marinated mushrooms and all the veggies and seasonings (except the remaining sesame oil and sesame seeds).

To soften the rice noodles, simply place in a bowl of boiled water. Once soft, drain the water and let the noodles continue to drain through a sieve until ready to use. You won't need to use much of the dried package, less

Preheat the oven to 350°F (176°C). To make the rolls, take 3-4 tablespoons of the filling and place it in the centre of one wrapper, about an inch from the top. Working from the top, start to roll the wrapper, tucking in the sides as you go, wrapping fairly securely but not so tight that it tears the wrapper. (If it does tear, just save the filling, discard the wrapper, and use a new one.) Place the roll seam side down on a baking tray or in an 8"x12" (or larger) baking dish lined with parchment paper. Repeat this process until you have used all the filling. Lightly brush the tops of the rolls with the toasted sesame oil, and sprinkle with the optional toasted sesame seeds. Bake for 26-30 minutes, until golden. Serve with a plum sauce, peanut sauce, or Ginger Dipping Sauce (p. 49)

Makes 15-20 rolls.

than ¼ of most brands. Once softened, measure out 1½ - 1¾ cups.

You can use other veggies in these rolls to replace some of the carrot and/or celery, such as red or yellow bell peppers. If you want to make them a little more substantial, you could add some marinated and sautéed tofu, toasted sesame seeds, or some hemp seed nuts to the filling.

Chipotle Veggie-Bean Burritos

Wheat-Free Option

These burritos are smoky and spicy, and packed with corn, beans, and veggies. Be sure to serve topped with Creamy Avocado Cashew Sauce (p. 46), and pair with a salad dressed with Cumin Lime Vinaigrette (p. 48).

1 28-oz can	(796-ml) diced tomatoes, drained (see note)
1 - 1½ tbsp	olive oil
¾ cup	red onion, finely chopped
2	large cloves garlic, minced or pressed
½ tsp	sea salt
	freshly ground black pepper to taste
2 tsp	chipotle hot sauce (see note)
1 tsp	chile powder
1 tsp	cumin
1 tsp	mustard seed
½ tsp	dried oregano
½ tsp	dried basil
1 cup	green bell pepper, diced
⅓ cup	celery, diced
1 cup	cooked beans of choice (e.g., black beans, adzuki beans)
⅓ - ½ cup	frozen corn kernels
½ tsp	honey alternative
6	large (10") flour tortillas (see note)
1 - 1½ cup	grated non-dairy mozzarella cheese (optional)

Press the drained tomatoes to remove as much liquid as possible. Set aside ¾ cup of the tomatoes. In a large skillet over medium heat, heat the oil. Add the onion, garlic, salt, pepper, chipotle hot sauce, and all the dried spices and herbs. Stir through for 5-6 minutes, then add in the green pepper and celery, and stir through for another couple of minutes. Stir in the remaining ingredients, including the diced tomatoes (except the reserved portion). Cook for a few minutes, then remove from heat and let cool.

Preheat oven to 375°F (190°C). Spoon about ⅙ of the cooled filling into each of the tortillas, leaving a few inches around each edge. Bring the bottom edge over top of the filling, and begin to roll up the burrito, tucking in the sides as you go until fully rolled.

Muir Glen Fire Roasted Tomatoes lend a natural smoky flavor here, but if you can't find them, regular diced tomatoes are just fine.

Place the burritos, folded side down, in a lightly oiled 8"x12" (or similar) baking dish. Sprinkle the reserved diced tomatoes over top of the burritos. Cover with foil and bake for 15-17 minutes. Remove foil, sprinkle on the optional soy cheese, and bake uncovered for another 5-7 minutes until the tops have browned lightly and the cheese is melted.

Makes 6 burritos.

You can use another kind of hot sauce, but the flavor and intensity will be different; chipotle hot sauce imparts a deep, smoky flavor with some heat, not a fiery hot intensity.

Use spelt or other wheat-free tortillas for a wheat-free version.

Curried Rice 'n' Bean-Filled Zucchini

Wheat-Free

I love this dish; it's yummy, and has lots of texture – chewy grains, soft beans and rice, and crunchy cashews. Plus, if you use leftover whole grains and beans on hand (see Guide to Cooking Beans, p. 165), it can be prepared super fast!

1 cup	cooked adzuki or black beans (or other small bean)
1 cup	cooked chewy grain (e.g., whole kamut, spelt, wheat berries)
1 cup	cooked brown rice (see note)
½ cup	celery, diced
½ cup	green onions, chopped
¼ cup	tahini
2 - 3 tbsp	raisins
1 tbsp	mild curry paste
½ - ¾ tsp	blackstrap molasses
¼ tsp	cumin
¼ tsp	sea salt
⅛ tsp	cinnamon
2	medium-large zucchini (or 3 smaller)
4 - 5 tbsp	cashews, crushed or ground a little

Preheat oven to 375°F (190°C). In a large bowl, combine all the ingredients except the zucchini and cashews. Mix well to bind the mixture. Trim the ends off the zucchini and split lengthwise. Use a spoon to scoop out seeds and some flesh the whole length of zucchini, leaving about ¼ - ½" of flesh. Discard scrapings. Place zucchini halves in a lightly oiled 8"x12" (or similar) baking dish. Spoon mixture into zucchini, heaping the filling in each, and sprinkle with the cashews. Cover with foil and bake for 23-25 minutes, then remove foil and bake for another 12-14 minutes.

Makes 4 servings.

Short-grain brown rice works well, because it's a little sticky, but you could also use brown basmati rice, wild rice, or other grains like millet, quinoa, or barley. You can also mix the rice and grains for a total of 2 cups. A chewy grain like kamut adds nice texture, but 2 cups of leftover rice works perfectly fine too!

This dish is great drizzled with a dressing or vinaigrette. Try the Lemon Zinger Vinaigrette (p. 51), Balsamic-Garlic Flax Oil (p. 44), or Lemon Curry Vinaigrette, on page 78 of my first cookbook, *The Everyday Vegan*.

Gram's Zesty Tomato Sauce

Charlotte's "Gram" came up with this tomato sauce and uses it for spaghetti, lasagna, and in casseroles as well as in cabbage rolls (which she fills with a pilaf made from brown rice, couscous, onions, and other seasonings). This recipe makes a large batch, so you can freeze some!

1 tbsp	olive oil
1	medium onion, chopped
4	medium-large cloves garlic, minced
1 tsp	dried basil
1 tsp	dried oregano
½ tsp	dried thyme
¼ tsp	sea salt (generous)
	freshly ground black pepper to taste
2 cups	white mushrooms, sliced
1 25.5-oz jar	(750-ml) (or similar) good quality pasta sauce
1 28-oz can	(796-ml) diced tomatoes
1 cup	chili sauce
1 15-oz can	(396-ml) kidney beans (or other bean of choice), rinsed and drained (see note)
1 12-oz pkg	(340-g) (or similar) veggie ground round (Italian flavor is good) (see note)

In a large pot over medium heat, add the oil, onion, garlic, dried herbs, sea salt, and pepper. Cover and let cook for 3-4 minutes, stirring occasionally. Add the mushrooms and let cook uncovered for another few minutes. Add the pasta sauce, tomatoes, and chili sauce. Bring to a boil, then reduce heat, cover, and let simmer for 10 minutes. Add the beans and veggie ground round, cover, and let simmer for another 10-15 minutes. Serve over cooked spaghetti or other pasta noodles.

Makes 6 or more servings.

The beans and veggie ground round make a heartier sauce, but you can omit either or both if desired; you could also use 2 cans of beans (same or different types) in place of the veggie ground round.

For a wheat-free version, omit the veggie ground round.

Greek Basmati Rice

Wheat-Free

This is a piquant rice dish with some traditional Greek flavors that's quite easy to prepare, since the oven does most of the work for you. Try pairing with Lemon-Herb Tofu (p. 65) and a salad.

1½ cups	brown basmati rice, rinsed (see note)
3¼ cups	water
1 cup	red onion, diced
1 - 1¼ cup	tomatoes, chopped, seeds removed
2	medium-large cloves garlic, minced
2½ tbsp	extra-virgin olive oil
2½ tbsp	freshly squeezed lemon juice
2 tsp	dried oregano
¾ tsp	sea salt
	freshly ground black pepper to taste
½ - ¾ cup	pitted kalamata olives
1½ - 2 tbsp	fresh mint, chopped
⅓ - ½ cup	fresh parsley, chopped
	lemon wedges (to finish)

Preheat oven to 400°F (204°C). In a lightly oiled, deep casserole dish, combine all the ingredients except the olives, mint, and parsley and stir through to mix. Cover and bake for 60-65 minutes. Add the olives and stir through. Cover and bake for another 10-15 minutes or more, until the rice is soft and has absorbed all the water. Remove and stir in the fresh mint and parsley. Drizzle with extra olive oil and a squeeze of fresh lemon juice.

Makes 4-6 servings, depending on accompaniments.

You can use regular brown rice for this dish if you like. Brown basmati rice has a more buttery flavor, while regular brown rice is stickier.

Hummus Tortilla Pizzas

Wheat-Free
Option

I love the versatility of these pizzas – you can use your favorite veggies, and vary the quantities. If you have hummus and flour tortillas on hand, these make a fast, fun, and easy supper!

4	large (10") flour tortillas (see note)
3 - 3½ cups	zucchini, sliced into ¼" rounds (see note)
1 cup	red bell pepper, sliced (see note)
1½ tbsp	olive oil
1 - 2 tsp	hoisin sauce
½ tsp	ground fennel or coriander (or other seasonings you like)
¼ tsp	sea salt
	freshly ground black pepper to taste
⅓ - ½ cup	kalamata olives, pitted and sliced in half
½ cup	green onions, sliced
2 cups	hummus (use Creamy Hummus, p. 62, or Cannellini Bean Yam Hummus, p. 60, or other prepared hummus)
¼ cup	chopped parsley, basil, cilantro, or dill (optional, for garnish)

Preheat oven to 375°F (190°C). Place tortillas on a baking sheet lined with parchment paper. Bake for 5-8 minutes, until just crispy and golden. Remove from oven, reserve baking sheet, and set oven to grill/broil. In a bowl, toss the zucchini and red peppers with the olive oil, hoisin sauce, ground fennel or coriander, sea salt, and black pepper. Place on a lined baking sheet and broil for 7-8 minutes. Remove and reset oven to 375°F (190°C). Spread hummus over the tortillas, and distribute the zucchini, peppers, olives and green onions over each. Bake for 8-11 minutes until golden and heated through. Remove and sprinkle over optional herbs, and drizzle with Balsamic-Garlic Flax Oil (p. 44).

Makes 4 servings.

Use spelt or other wheat-free tortillas for a wheat-free version.

You can easily substitute other veggies for some or all of the zucchini and red pepper; try thinly sliced fennel, blanched broccoli flowerets, or sliced wild mushrooms. Marinated artichokes can also be used, but no grilling needed; just add with the olives.

Molasses Baked Beans

Wheat-Free

My mother makes wonderful baked beans, but she cooks from taste and experience, not from recipes. So I gathered what information I could and created a similar dish with less baking time. The result is tender, delicious, saucy baked beans. I hope you enjoy them, Mom!

2 cups	dry navy beans (roughly 1 lb/450 g), rinsed
20 cups	water (to boil beans twice)
2	large red onions (or 3 medium), roughly chopped (about 4½ cups)
3	cups water (for sauce)
½ cup	blackstrap molasses
½ cup	ketchup
3 tbsp	tamari
2 tbsp	apple cider vinegar
1 tbsp	curry powder
2 tsp	dry mustard
⅛ tsp	ground cloves
	freshly ground black pepper to taste
2	dried bay leaves

In a large pot over high heat, combine the beans with 10 cups of water. Bring to a boil, and let boil uncovered for 7-8 minutes (reduce heat if it begins to boil over). Drain and rinse beans and rinse cooking pot. Return beans to pot with another 10 cups of water. Bring to a boil, reduce heat, and cook on medium-low heat partially covered for 30-35 minutes. Drain and rinse beans once more. Preheat oven to 350°F (176°C). In a large casserole dish with a lid, combine the beans with the remaining ingredients. Cover and bake for 3½ hours, stirring occasionally, until the sauce has thickened and beans are tender. To thicken sauce more, remove lid and cook for another 15 minutes or more. Remove bay leaves and serve.

Makes 6-8 servings.

Use leftovers for burritos! Purée beans in a food processor with some cumin to taste (and other seasonings like hot sauce). Spread purée on flour tortillas, fill with some sauteed veggies, roll up into a burrito, top with a little chili sauce and non-dairy cheese, and bake! (See Chipotle Veggie-Bean Burritos, p. 90, for more details on burrito-making.)

Moroccan Chickpea Patties

Wheat-Free Option

This recipe shines with flavors that you probably haven't had in veggie patties, including fennel, ginger, and cinnamon. They're fabulous served on their own, along with a salad and maybe some oven baked fries or Chipotle Yam Wedges (p. 61). These patties are so moist you don't need a sauce, but if you want one, try the Ginger Dipping Sauce (p. 49) or Mi-So Good Gravy from *The Everyday Vegan*.

1 tbsp	olive oil	1½ tbsp	apple cider vinegar
1	medium fennel bulb, chopped (stalks and core discarded, roughly 1½ - 2 cups)	2 tbsp	olive oil (for purée)
		2 tsp	freshly grated ginger
		½ tsp	sea salt
⅛ tsp	sea salt	¼ tsp	cumin
	freshly ground black pepper to taste	¾ tsp	paprika
		⅛ tsp	cinnamon
		⅓ - ½ cup	sliced green onions
½ cup	red bell pepper, chopped	½ cup	good quality breadcrumbs (see note)
2 cups	cooked chickpeas (garbanzo beans)	3 tbsp	sesame seeds
1	medium clove garlic, chopped	⅛ tsp	sea salt
		1 tbsp	olive oil (for frying)

In a skillet over medium heat, heat the oil. Add the fennel, salt, and pepper and cook for 5-6 minutes. Add the red pepper and cook for another 5 minutes or until the fennel has softened. Remove from heat. In a food processor, combine the chickpeas with the garlic, vinegar, olive oil, ginger, salt, cumin, paprika, and cinnamon and purée until the mixture becomes smooth (scrape down the sides of the bowl as needed). If still a little chunky, add a touch more oil or water, and purée again until smooth. Transfer the mixture to a large bowl, and stir in the fennel/red pepper mixture and green onions. Stir through to combine well. If you have the time, refrigerate for at least an hour (the mixture will firm up and be easier to shape). Mix the breadcrumbs, sesame seeds, and sea salt, and pour onto a plate. Take a mound of the chickpea mixture (roughly ⅓ cup) and form patties, then dip both sides in the breadcrumb mixture. In a skillet over medium heat, heat the oil and fry the patties for about 7-9 minutes on each side, until lightly browned (flip only once or twice).

For a wheat-free version, make your own breadcrumbs using wheat-free bread.

Makes 7-9 patties.

Pumpkin Seed-Coated Lentil Patties

Wheat-Free Option

These patties have a mild curry taste and soft texture with a crispy pumpkin seed coating. Pair with a crunchy salad and maybe a side dish such as Chipotle Yam Wedges (p. 61) or Lemon Rosemary Potatoes (p. 66).

¾ cup	dry brown lentils
1½ cups	water
2	dried bay leaves
1 tsp	coriander seeds
2 cups	red onion, cut in chunks (1 large onion)
2	medium-large cloves garlic, chopped
½ tsp	sea salt
1½ tbsp	apple cider vinegar
1½ tbsp	mild curry paste
1½ cups	good quality breadcrumbs (see note)
¼ - ⅓ cup	celery, diced
⅓ - ½ cup	ground pumpkin seeds (see note)
2 tbsp	olive oil (for frying)

For a wheat-free version, make your own breadcrumbs using wheat-free bread.

To grind the pumpkin seeds, process whole seeds (dry roasted are good) in a food processor until just crumbly (not too long or they can become seed butter).

In a pot over medium-high heat, combine the lentils, water, bay leaves, and coriander seeds. Bring to a boil, reduce heat to low/medium-low, cover, and cook for about 15 minutes. Add the onions and garlic, stir through, cover, and cook for another 12-15 minutes, until the lentils and onions are soft and the water is absorbed. Remove bay leaves and discard. Transfer mixture to a food processor with the remaining ingredients (except celery and ground pumpkin seeds) and purée until fairly smooth. Transfer mixture to a large bowl and stir in the celery. Refrigerate for 1 hour or more if possible (the mixture will be firm up and be easier to shape). Place ground pumpkin seeds on a plate. Take scoops of the mixture (roughly ⅓ cup) and form patties, then dip into the ground pumpkin seeds. In a skillet over medium-high heat, heat the oil and fry patties for 5-8 minutes on each side until lightly browned and crispy (flip only once or twice). Serve drizzled with Ginger Dipping Sauce (p. 49), Balsamic-Garlic Flax Oil (p. 44), or some plum sauce on the side.

Makes 8-10 patties.

Puréed Chickpea Pasta Sauce with Fresh Herbs

While the list of ingredients here looks long, this is a quick and simple recipe. When tossed with cooked pasta, it makes a full-flavored, satisfying, and healthy meal!

2½ cups	cooked chickpeas (garbanzo beans) (see note)
1	medium-large clove garlic, chopped
3 tbsp	sunflower oil (or extra-virgin olive oil)
2 tbsp	apple cider vinegar
1 - 2 tbsp	freshly squeezed lemon juice
1½ - 2 tbsp	mild miso (e.g., brown rice miso)
1 tbsp	tamari
1 tsp	dry mustard
½ tsp	honey alternative
½ tsp	vegan worcestershire sauce
½ tsp	dried oregano
¼ tsp	sea salt
¼ tsp	turmeric
1¼ cups	plain non-dairy milk (or more to taste) (see note)
½ cup	green onions, chopped (mostly green portion)
⅓ - ½ cup	fresh parsley, roughly chopped (optional)
1½ - 2 tbsp	fresh oregano or thyme, roughly chopped

If you want to thin out the sauce, add more non-dairy milk, up to an extra ½ cup. Also, after the pasta has been sitting for 5 or more minutes, it will absorb much of the sauce, so you may need to add more milk and/or a little oil.

You can replace the chickpeas with another light color bean (such as cannellini or black-eyed peas). But note that they will be creamier in texture than chickpeas, so you may not need as much non-dairy milk for the sauce. Start with 1 cup, and adjust to taste when combined with the pasta.

I like to use a light pasta with this sauce, such as rice vermicelli or fettucine. Soba noodles also work well, as do pastas made from rice or vegetable blends. Roughly 1 lb (450 g) of pasta works well with this recipe; when pasta is ready, drain lightly (let some of the water cling to the noodles) and toss in the sauce for a few minutes off the heat on the stove. Drizzle with sunflower or olive oil and be sure to serve with lemon wedges.

In a blender or food processor, combine all the ingredients (except the non-dairy milk, green onions, optional parsley, and fresh oregano or thyme) and purée until very smooth (stop to scrape down the sides of the bowl as needed). Add the milk and purée again until you have a very smooth consistency. Add the herbs and green onions and pulse until just incorporated (do not purée them). Toss sauce into cooked pasta and serve (see note).

Makes 4 servings.

Roasted Pepper Cannellini Bean Sauce

Wheat-Free

This full-bodied sauce is quick and wonderful over a whole grain like quinoa, wild rice, or a light pasta. Keep cooked cannellini beans on hand (see Guide to Cooking Beans, p. 165), a jar of roasted red peppers, and you're set!

1 cup	vegetable stock
3 - 4	medium-large cloves garlic, minced
½ tsp	dried thyme or oregano
good pinch	dried sage
2 - 2½ cups	cooked cannellini beans (see note)
1 tsp	fresh rosemary, finely chopped (see note)
⅛ - ¼ tsp	sea salt (season to taste depending on saltiness of veggie stock)
	freshly ground black pepper to taste
1 - 1½ cups	roasted red peppers, roughly chopped (see Cooking Notes, p. 167)
3 - 4 tbsp	toasted pine nuts (see Cooking Notes, p. 167)
2 tbsp	extra-virgin olive oil (or more, if desired)
2 - 3 tsp	balsamic vinegar

In a large skillet over medium heat, add the veggie stock, garlic, and dried herbs, and cook for 4-5 minutes, until the garlic just softens. Add the cannellini beans, rosemary, sea salt (start with ⅛ tsp), and black pepper. Cover and cook for 6-7 minutes, stirring occasionally, until the beans start to break up and dissolve into the sauce. Remove cover and stir in the roasted red peppers and pine nuts. If serving immediately, also stir in the olive oil and balsamic vinegar; if not, turn off heat and cover. Just before serving, warm through again, and add the olive oil and vinegar.

Makes 4 servings.

Cannellini beans are excellent here; they are soft and melt into the sauce. If you don't have them, though, you can use another white bean, or chickpeas.

If you don't have fresh rosemary, use about ½ tsp of dried. Crush or crumble in your fingers a little then add it right at the beginning of the recipe, along with the garlic and other dried herbs.

Rosemary Seasoned Tofu Balls

A little fresh rosemary goes a long way in these moist and flavorful tofu balls. Serve with sauce on top of pasta or a whole grain, along with a light salad.

7 oz	(200 g) firm/extra-firm tofu, squeezed dry and broken in chunks (use fresh, do not freeze and thaw) (roughly 1½ cups)	1½ tsp	Dijon mustard	
		1½ tbsp	olive oil	
		⅛ tsp	sea salt	
			freshly ground black pepper to taste	
2 tbsp	miso	½ cup	red or orange bell pepper, chopped	
1 tbsp	apple cider vinegar			
2	medium-large clove garlic, chopped	¾ cup	green onions, chopped	
		3 cups	good quality breadcrumbs	
1 tbsp	fresh rosemary, roughly chopped			
		2 tsp	olive oil (for baking sheet)	
1½ tbsp	ketchup			
1 tbsp	vegetarian Worcestershire sauce			

In a blender or food processor, purée tofu until crumbly. Add the miso, vinegar, garlic, rosemary, ketchup, Worcestershire sauce, mustard, olive oil, salt, and pepper, and purée until smooth and thick (stop to scrape down the sides of the bowl as needed). Add the red pepper and green onions and pulse through until well combined, but keeping some texture. Transfer to a bowl and stir in the breadcrumbs; the mixture should be soft but hold together when pressed. Preheat oven to 375°F (190°C). Line a baking sheet with parchment paper, and drizzle on the olive oil. Scoop golf-ball sized portions of the mixture, form into balls, and place on the baking sheet. Bake for 20-25 minutes, until golden. Top with the pasta sauce below and Balsamic-Garlic Flax Oil (p. 44).

Makes 20-24 balls.

Sauce:

1 - 1¼ cups	good quality tomato pasta sauce
1 tbsp	balsamic vinegar
1 - 1½ tsp	honey alternative
1 tsp	vegan Worcestershire sauce

In a saucepan over medium heat, combine all the ingredients and stir until heated through.

Scalloped Potatoes

Wheat-Free Option

I fondly remember scalloped potatoes from my childhood. My mom often made them for guests, as well as for our family of eight! It couldn't have been easy trying to please six growing girls every night at dinner, but scalloped potatoes always did the trick. This version is velvety and creamy, with a little more "zing" than traditional recipes.

Potato Layer:

3 cups	plain non-dairy milk
1	large clove garlic
¼ cup	miso
3 tbsp	arrowroot powder
2 tbsp	whole wheat pastry flour (see note)
2 tbsp	olive oil
2 tsp	Dijon mustard
1 tsp	dried rosemary
¼ - ½ tsp	honey alternative (e.g., barley malt or fruit syrup)
¼ tsp	sea salt
⅛ - ¼ tsp	freshly grated nutmeg
few pinches	freshly ground pepper
2 lbs	(1 kg) Yukon or red potatoes, thinly sliced (skins optional)
1½ - 2 cups	red onion, very thinly sliced (1 medium red onion)

Topping:

2 cups	good quality breadcrumbs (see note)
2 tbsp	olive oil
⅛ tsp	sea salt

In a blender or food processor, prepare the sauce by combining 1 cup of milk with the garlic, miso, arrowroot, flour, olive oil, mustard, rosemary, honey alternative, salt, nutmeg, and pepper and blend until uniform. Add the remaining 2 cups of milk and blend through again. Preheat oven to 400°F (204°C). In a lightly oiled 8"x12" casserole dish, place a layer of potatoes (⅓ of total), followed by a layer of ½ of the onions. Repeat process, finishing with a final layer of potatoes. Pour the milk mixture over top and cover (if using aluminum foil, loosely cover to keep off the potatoes). Bake for 50-60 minutes, until potatoes can be pierced with a knife; place a tray (lined with parchment for easy cleaning) on a lower rack to catch drippings.

For a wheat-free version, use spelt flour and make your own breadcrumbs using wheat-free bread.

In a bowl, combine the topping ingredients, working through with your fingers. When potatoes are ready, sprinkle on the topping and bake uncovered for 7-10 minutes until lightly browned. Remove from heat and let sit for 5-10 minutes before serving.

Makes 5-6 servings.

Sunflower-Lentil Pie

This comforting, earthy dish is much like a loaf, but baked in a pie dish so that it's easier to cut. Definitely serve it drizzled with Sesame Mustard Tahini Sauce (p. 56) or Balsamic-Garlic Flax Oil (p. 44), along with a crunchy salad.

¾ cup	brown lentils
1¾ cups	water
1½ cups	red onion, roughly chopped
1 cup	quick oats
½ cup	sunflower seeds
½ cup	celery, chopped
1	medium-large clove garlic, roughly chopped
2 tbsp	ketchup
2 tbsp	tamari
1 tbsp	balsamic vinegar
2 tsp	vegan Worcestershire sauce
½ tsp	dried rosemary
1 tsp	dried oregano
⅛ tsp	sea salt
	freshly ground black pepper to taste

In a large pot over medium-high heat, combine the lentils and water and bring to a boil. Reduce heat to medium-low, cover, and let cook for 15-20 minutes. Add the onions, stir through, and let cook for another 10-15 minutes, covered, until the lentils are soft and have absorbed all the water. In a blender or food processor, combine the lentil mixture with the remaining ingredients and purée until just smooth, but retaining some texture. Transfer mixture to a lightly oiled pie plate, and distribute evenly. Bake at 375°F (190°C) for 27-30 minutes, until lightly browned and just firm. Let stand for a few minutes (it will firm more as it cools), then slice into wedges.

Makes 5-6 servings, depending on accompaniments.

Mash leftovers of this loaf mixed with a little vegan mayonnaise for a savory sandwich filling!

Sunny Southwestern Squash Pizzas

Wheat-Free Option

A delightful twist on a tortilla pizza using orange winter squash. Give it a try; it's fun and delicious!

4	large (10") flour tortillas
1 tbsp	olive oil
2 cups	red onions, halved and thinly sliced
	freshly ground black pepper to taste
2 tsp	tamari
1 - 1¼ cups	red bell pepper, thinly sliced (roughly 1 medium pepper)
2 cups	cooked dark orange squash (e.g., butternut, buttercup, kabocha) (see note)
1	small clove garlic, chopped
3 tbsp	apple cider vinegar
3 tbsp	plain non-dairy milk
2 tbsp	olive oil
⅓ cup	fresh parsley, chopped
½ tsp	cumin
½ tsp	sea salt
¼ tsp	honey alternative
¼ tsp	chipotle hot sauce
⅛ tsp	chili powder
½ - ¾ cup	cooked black beans or adzuki beans
½ cup	frozen corn kernels
½ cup	grated non-dairy cheese (optional)

Preheat oven to 375°F (190°C). Place tortillas on a baking sheet lined with parchment paper and bake for 5-8 minutes, until just crispy and golden (not browned). Remove from oven and let cool. In a large skillet over medium heat, heat the oil. Add the onions and a few pinches of pepper and cook uncovered for 7-8 minutes. Add the tamari and red peppers, stir through, and continue to cook for another 6-8 minutes, until onions are soft. Remove from heat and let cool. While cooking/cooling onions, you can prepare squash mixture. In a food processor, combine the squash, garlic, vinegar, non-dairy milk, olive oil, parsley, cumin, sea salt, honey

For a wheat-free version, use spelt or other wheat-free tortillas.

To roast the squash, place on a baking sheet lined with parchment paper. Bake at 400°F (204°C) for 40-60 minutes or more, depending on size of squash(es). Once soft and alternative, chipotle sauce, and chili powder, and purée until very smooth (stop to scrape down the sides of the bowl as needed). Once tortilla shells are cool, spread the squash mixture evenly over each. Spread the onions and peppers over top, followed by the beans, corn, and optional cheese. Bake at 375°F (190°C) for 11-14 minutes, until golden. To serve, drizzle with a little extra-virgin olive oil or Balsamic-Garlic Flax Oil (p. 44).

Makes 4 servings (or more as a side dish or appetizer).

easily pierced, remove from oven and let cool before handling. Slice in half, discard seeds and pulp, and scoop out squash flesh. Freeze any extra in 2-cup portions; If using frozen, drain any excess water/liquid from the squash once thawed.

Sweet Curry Chickpea Casserole

Wheat-Free

A rich and scrumptious stew. It's a little creamy with a curry flavor that's not too hot, and a natural sweetness from the coconut milk, sweet potatoes, and apples. Serve with a salad and alongside a cooked grain such as quinoa, wild rice, or brown rice, or some hearty bread.

2½ - 3 cups	cooked chickpeas (garbanzo beans)
1 13.5-oz can	(400-ml) light coconut milk
¾ cup	red onion, chopped
1½ cups	celery, chopped
1 - 1½ cups	sweet potatoes (not yams), peeled and chopped
1 - 1½ cups	apple, peeled and chopped
2	small-medium cloves garlic, minced
1½ tbsp	freshly grated ginger
1 - 1½ tbsp	mild curry paste (the more you use, the hotter it will be)
2 tsp	mustard seeds
1 tsp	cumin seeds
½ tsp	turmeric
¾ tsp	sea salt
⅛ tsp	allspice

Preheat oven to 375°F (190°C). In a large, deep casserole dish, combine all the ingredients. Stir through until well combined. Cover and bake for 30 minutes. Stir through, cover, and bake for another 30-40 minutes, until the vegetables are tender (stir through again once or twice throughout).

Makes 4-5 servings, depending on accompaniments.

The coconut milk gives this dish a richer taste and doesn't separate while cooking as a non-dairy milk can. But if you don't have coconut milk on hand, or prefer not to use it, you can use 1¼ - 1½ cups of a non-dairy milk. If so, add a tablespoon of olive oil for a little added richness.

Tomato-Lentil Pasta Sauce

Wheat-Free

This sauce is deceiving; it has such a robust flavor, you'd expect it would have a long list of ingredients. But the truth is it's basic, fast, and just plain wonderful! Toss it with a healthy pasta like a soba/kamut noodle or rice noodle, and pair it with a light salad for a nutritious meal.

2 tbsp	olive oil
½ tsp	sea salt
1 tsp	dried oregano
½ tsp	dried basil
½ tsp	dried thyme
½ tsp	dried rosemary
	freshly ground black pepper to taste
4	medium cloves garlic, minced
½ cup	red or white wine
1 28-oz can	(796-ml) diced tomatoes
½ cup	brown lentils, rinsed
⅔ - ¾ cup	water
3 tbsp	capers, rinsed and drained
3 - 4 tbsp	toasted pine nuts (see Cooking Notes, p. 167)
	or hemp seed nuts (garnish) (optional)
	non-dairy parmesan (garnish) (optional)

In a large pot over medium heat, add the olive oil, salt, dried herbs, pepper, and garlic, and cook for a few minutes until the garlic has softened (reduce heat if garlic starts to brown). Add the wine, increase heat to high, and bring to a boil for a couple of minutes. Add the tomatoes, lentils, and water, and let the mixture come to a boil again. Reduce heat to medium-low, cover, and let cook for 35-40 minutes, until the lentils are soft. Turn off heat until pasta is ready. After tossing with pasta (see note), add the capers and toss through, season to taste with additional salt and pepper, and garnish with toasted pine nuts, a drizzle of extra-virgin olive oil, and non-dairy parmesan if desired.

Makes 4 or more servings.

Use about 1 lb (450 g) of dry pasta for this sauce. While cooking the pasta, reserve a cup or so of the cooking water. Once pasta is ready, drain, and toss through the lentil sauce with a little of the pasta water.

Veggie Stirfry with Spicy Almond Sauce

Wheat-Free

A stirfry doesn't get much more appetizing than this one! The sautéed tofu and vegetables are smothered with a creamy-spicy sauce made with almond butter (much like a peanut sauce). Eat on its own or on top of quinoa, brown basmati rice, or another whole grain!

Tofu Marinade:

2 tbsp	rice vinegar or apple cider vinegar
2 tbsp	tamari
1 10-12-oz pkg	(300-350-g) firm or extra-firm tofu, excess water squeezed out, and cubed (roughly 2½ - 3 cups, cubed)

Almond Sauce:

½ cup	almond butter
1 cup	plain soy milk or other non-dairy milk
⅓ cup	unseasoned rice vinegar or apple cider vinegar
1	large clove garlic, roughly chopped
3 tbsp	tamari
2 - 2½ tbsp	fresh ginger, roughly chopped
1 tbsp	toasted sesame oil
¼ - ½ tsp	crushed red pepper

Veggie Sauté:

1 tbsp	olive oil (½ to sauté tofu, ½ to sauté veggies)
1 cup	red onion, chopped
few pinches	sea salt
	freshly ground black pepper to taste
1 cup	celery, thinly sliced (on diagonal)
1 cup	zucchini, quartered and sliced ¼" thick
2½ - 3 cups	broccoli flowerets (approx. 1 head of broccoli)
3 - 3½ cups	white button mushrooms, quartered or halved, depending on size
1 - 1½ cups	red bell pepper, cored and chopped
1 bunch	Swiss chard, stems removed and leaves roughly chopped
	lemon wedges (to finish)

For the tofu marinade: In a large bowl, combine the rice vinegar and tamari. Add the cubed tofu, toss to coat, and let marinate.

For the almond sauce: In a blender or food processor, combine all the ingredients and purée until smooth.

For the sauté: In a deep skillet or pot over medium-high heat, heat ½ tbsp of the olive oil. Add the marinated tofu and sauté for 6-8 minutes, tossing occasionally, until lightly browned. Remove tofu and set aside, and reserve skillet. Over medium heat, heat the remaining olive oil. Add the onions, sea salt, and black pepper, cover, and let cook for a few minutes. Add the celery, zucchini, broccoli, and mushrooms, cover, and let cook for about 5 minutes, stirring occasionally. Add the red peppers and let cook another couple of minutes. Once the broccoli is bright green and just tender, stir in the almond sauce and Swiss chard, followed by the tofu. Cover and let cook 2-3 minutes, stirring occasionally, until the Swiss chard has just wilted (do not let sit too long or the chard and broccoli will overcook). Serve on top of quinoa, wild or brown basmati rice, or rice noodles, with a squeeze of fresh lemon juice.

Makes 4-5 servings.

Vicki's Hummus-Quinoa Casserole

Wheat-Free

My friend Vicki enjoys quinoa and asked for some different ways to use it. This casserole showcases quinoa as more than a side dish alternative to rice, and is simple and quick to prepare if you have some hummus on hand.

1	fennel bulb, core/stalks removed, halved and thinly sliced (1½ cups) (see note)
1	large zucchini (or 2 small), sliced thin in rounds (2½ - 3 cups) (see note)
1	small-medium red or yellow bell pepper, cored and thinly sliced (1 cup) (see note)
1½ - 2 tbsp	olive oil
1½ - 2 tsp	balsamic vinegar
¼ tsp	sea salt
	freshly ground black pepper to taste
2½ - 3 cups	cooked quinoa (see note)
2 cups	hummus (Creamy Hummus, p. 62, Cannellini Bean Yam Hummus, p. 60, or a prepared hummus)
3 - 4 tbsp	fresh parsley, basil, or coriander, chopped (optional)

Preheat oven to 450°F (232°C). In a large bowl, toss the fennel, zucchini, and red pepper with the olive oil, balsamic vinegar, salt, and pepper. Transfer veggies to a baking sheet lined with parchment paper and bake for 15-18 minutes, until golden in spots. Remove and begin to assemble your casserole. Reset oven to 375°F (190°C). In a lightly oiled 8"x12" (or similar) baking dish, spread the cooked quinoa evenly over the base and press it down gently. Drop spoonfuls of the hummus over the quinoa, and lightly spread to distribute evenly (try to avoid breaking up the layers). Distribute the roasted veggies over the hummus and bake for 20-25 minutes. Remove and sprinkle with the fresh herbs if desired. Drizzle with extra olive oil or Balsamic-Garlic Flax Oil (p. 44).

Makes 4-6 servings.

You can substitute other veggies here, depending on what you like or have on hand. Try sliced mushrooms, thinly sliced eggplant, or lightly blanched broccoli flowerets. Add some sliced kalamata olives for a zesty punch!

To yield this amount of cooked quinoa, rinse 1 cup quinoa and combine with 2 cups water and a few pinches of sea salt in a saucepan. Bring to a boil, reduce heat, and let simmer covered for about 13-15 minutes until cooked.

Walnut Basil Pesto

When basil is in season, be sure to make this awesome pesto! The toasted walnuts add extra flavor to the basil, garlic, and lemon, as well as a crunchy texture. It's a satisfying, tasty pesto that's creamy and nutty rather than oily.

1 cup	toasted walnuts (see Cooking Notes, p. 167)
1¼ cups	plain non-dairy milk
1	medium-large clove garlic
1½ tbsp	tamari
2 tbsp	cashew butter (or tahini)
2 - 3 tbsp	freshly squeezed lemon juice
1 tsp	Dijon mustard
½ tsp	sea salt
	freshly ground black pepper to taste
2 cups	(packed) fresh basil (leaves only)

In a blender or food processor, combine the walnuts, milk, garlic, tamari, cashew butter, lemon juice, mustard, salt, and pepper, and purée until mixed (does not have to be smooth) (stop to scrape down the sides of the bowl as needed). Add the basil and pulse to purée, scraping the sides of the bowl again as needed. Season to taste with additional sea salt and black pepper, and toss with cooked pasta (see note).

Makes 3-4 servings with pasta.

About ¾ to 1 lb (400 to 450 g) of pasta will serve 3-4 people nicely with this sauce – a rice, veggie, or kamut pasta is good. Once tossed with pesto, drizzle with extra-virgin olive oil to taste and several squeezes of fresh lemon juice, and sprinkle with non-dairy parmesan if desired. This can also be served over a cooked grain, such as quinoa, or brown rice.

Sweets

& Treats

Apple Cardamom Cake with Lemon-Maple Frosting

This delightful cake has become a favorite with family and friends. The cake is moist and flavorful, and the icing is creamy, sweet, and a little tangy, creating a luscious combination. Be sure to make it for your next special occasion!

Cake:

1¼ cup	unbleached all-purpose flour (see note)
¾ cup	ground oats (see Cooking Notes, p. 167)
¾ cup	unrefined sugar
2½ tsp	baking powder
1 tsp	baking soda
1½ tsp	cardamom
¼ tsp	cinnamon
¼ tsp	freshly grated nutmeg
¼ tsp	sea salt
1 cup	unsweetened applesauce
¾ cup	vanilla or plain non-dairy milk
2 tsp	pure vanilla extract
¼ cup	canola oil

Preheat oven to 350°F (176°C). In a large bowl, combine all the dry ingredients, sifting in the flour, baking powder, and baking soda. Stir through until well combined. In a separate bowl, combine the applesauce, non-dairy milk, vanilla, and oil. Add the wet mixture to the dry and stir through, mixing until just well combined (do not overmix). Pour into two lightly oiled cake pans (I use round pans) and bake for 22-24 minutes, until lightly golden and a toothpick inserted in the center comes out clean. Let cool completely before frosting.

For a wheat-free option, use spelt flour, but add another ¼ cup (for 1½ cups total).

Frosting:

1 12-oz pkg	(349-g) silken firm tofu (e.g., Mori-Nu brand)
1½ tsp	pure vanilla extract
2 tbsp	canola oil
⅓ cup	pure maple syrup
½ cup + 1 tbsp	unrefined sugar
⅛ tsp	sea salt
1½ tbsp	freshly squeezed lemon juice
1½ - 2 tsp	lemon rind (from approx. 1 lemon), reserve about ½ tsp
¼ cup	plain non-dairy milk
1 tbsp	agar powder

Pat the tofu dry with a paper towel to remove excess moisture. In a blender or food processor, purée the tofu and vanilla until smooth (stop to scrape down the sides of the bowl as needed). In a small saucepan over low heat, combine the canola oil with the maple syrup, sugar and salt, stirring occasionally until it starts to come together and the sugar dissolves. Add the lemon juice and lemon rind (reserving ½ tsp), again stirring occasionally. While this is warming, in a small bowl, combine the milk with the agar, and stir through until dissolved and smooth. Add this mixture to the maple syrup mixture, and stir through. Increase the heat to medium-high and while stirring, let it thicken and reach a boil. Reduce heat to low and let simmer for a couple of minutes to fully dissolve the agar. Remove from heat and add to the blender or food processor with the tofu, and purée. Add the reserved lemon rind and continue to blend until smooth (stop to scrape down the sides of the bowl as needed). Refrigerate until completely cool. When ready to use, reblend the tofu mixture, puréeing until completely smooth (see note). Frost your cake and refrigerate for at least a few hours to set. Serve cake slices with some vanilla or chocolate non-dairy ice-cream.

Makes 8 servings.

After chilling the tofu frosting, you may think you have made a mistake because it gels and becomes thick. But don't panic! After several minutes of puréeing, the frosting will smooth out; the longer you process it, the smoother it will become. If the frosting has become too thick, and is not smoothing out after being processed for a few minutes, add a tablespoon or two of non-dairy milk and purée again. Don't add too much, though, as the cream must be thick or it won't hold on the cake.

Apple Phyllo Strudel

Wheat-Free Option

Layers of paper-thin phyllo pastry make this version of a strudel light and crispy. The filling has generous chunks of apples that are lightly spiced and sweetened. Pair with non-dairy ice cream if you like, or serve on its own!

4½ cups	apples, peeled, cut from the core in 4 sections, and thinly sliced
1½ tbsp	freshly squeezed lemon juice
⅓ cup	unrefined sugar
2 tbsp	unbleached all-purpose flour (see note)
¾ tsp	cinnamon
⅛ - ¼ tsp	fresh grated nutmeg
⅛ tsp	allspice
⅛ tsp	sea salt
10	sheets phyllo pastry (see note)
3 tbsp	canola oil (or more/less as needed, for brushing the sheets)
2 - 3 tbsp	unrefined sugar (garnish)

For a wheat-free option, use spelt flour.

To keep the phyllo sheets that you're not currently working on from drying out, place a damp (not wet) dish towel over them.

You can also include ¼ cup or so of toasted chopped nuts (see Cooking Notes, p. 167) such as pecans or walnuts to the mixture, or for some decadence, some non-dairy chocolate chips!

Preheat oven to 350°F (176°C). In a large mixing bowl, combine the apples with the lemon juice as you slice them. Add the remaining ingredients (except the phyllo pastry sheets, canola oil, and extra unrefined sugar), and toss through to evenly coat the apples. On a baking sheet lined with parchment paper, place a phyllo sheet and brush lightly with the canola oil. Place another phyllo sheet on top and repeat until you've used all the phyllo sheets (you don't need to brush oil on the top sheet that you will be placing the apple mixture on); after every 2-3 sheets, sprinkle a little unrefined sugar over top.

Once you have used all the phyllo, place the apple mixture along the length (longest edge) of the phyllo, leaving about 1 inch from the edges and a couple of inches from the top. Take the bottom of the phyllo and begin to roll the pastry, holding the apple mixture in and tucking it as you go, pushing in the sides to encase the filling as you roll. Once rolled, brush more oil over top of the pastry, and sprinkle with a little more sugar. Bake for 27-30 minutes, remove and let cool before slicing. Serve as is or, even better, with some vanilla soy ice cream.

Makes 5-6 servings.

Banana Hazelnut Cream Pie

This pie has a smooth, velvety filling with a light banana taste in a toasted hazelnut-crumb crust. The flavors are exquisite!

Crust:

1 cup	**graham cracker or arrowroot cookie crumbs (see note)**
½ cups	**ground toasted hazelnuts, skins removed (see Cooking Notes, p. 167) (see note)**
⅛ tsp	**sea salt**
2½ - 3 tbsp	**canola oil**
3 - 3½ tbsp	**thick honey alternative (e.g., brown rice syrup or barley malt)**

Filling:

1 12-oz pkg	**(349-g) silken-firm tofu**
¾ cup	**plain non-dairy milk**
1 cup	**(fairly packed) ripe banana, sliced**
⅓ cup	**unrefined sugar**
3 tbsp	**pure maple syrup**
¼ cup	**(scant) unbleached all-purpose flour**
1 tbsp	**flaxmeal**
1 tbsp	**hazelnut syrup**
1½ tsp	**pure vanilla extract**
1½ - 2 tbsp	**freshly squeezed lemon juice**
¼ tsp	**sea salt**
⅛ tsp	**ground cardamom**

For the crust: In a bowl, combine the cracker or cookie crumbs, ground hazelnuts, and salt, and mix until well combined. Add the canola oil and honey alternative. Mix through well and then use your fingers to work the ingredients together, forming a crumbly mixture that will hold together somewhat when pressed. Transfer the mixture to a large pie plate, and press it around the sides and bottom.

For the filling: Preheat oven to 350°F (176°C). In a blender or food processor, purée the tofu until very smooth (stop to scrape the sides of the bowl as needed). Add the milk and bananas and purée again, then add the remaining ingredients and purée until smooth, scraping the bowl again as needed. Pour the filling into the pie crust. Bake the pie for 32-35 minutes, until mostly set (the centre will be a little loose, but will firm and set as it cools). Let cool completely. Serve as is or topped with some fresh berries, sorbet, or non-dairy ice cream, and drizzled with Easy Caramel Sauce (p. 127).

Makes 7-8 servings.

Use a blender or food processor to grind cookies and hazelnuts into crumbs (you can leave some texture to the hazelnuts).

You can use this crust as a base for other pie fillings. If your filling doesn't need to be baked, such as non-dairy ice-cream or pudding, then prebake the crust (at about 350°F (176°C) for 9-12 minutes).

Caramel Pecan Ice Cream Pan Cake

This frozen dessert is divine, combining vanilla cake, caramel sauce, toasted pecans, and your choice of non-dairy ice cream. It can be made in advance and kept in the freezer – but it won't last long there once you taste it!

Cake Layer:

1 cup	unbleached all-purpose flour
½ cup	unrefined sugar
1½ tsp	baking powder
¼ tsp	baking soda
¼ tsp	sea salt
¾ cup	plain soy milk
¼ cup	unsweetened applesauce
1 tsp	pure vanilla extract
¼ - ½ tsp	freshly squeezed lemon juice
3 tbsp	canola oil

Topping:

1 batch	Easy Caramel Sauce, cooled (see p. 127)
5 - 6 cups	vanilla soy ice cream (or other flavor, roughly 1⅓ 946-ml containers)
¼ - ⅓ cup	toasted pecans, lightly crushed (see Cooking Notes, p. 167)
2	medium or 1 large ripe banana, sliced
10 - 12	whole toasted pecans or handful of crushed (optional)

Preheat oven to 350°F (176°C).

For the cake: In a large bowl, combine the dry cake ingredients, sifting in the flour, baking powder, and baking soda. Mix until well combined. In a separate bowl, combine the wet cake ingredients. Add the wet mixture to the dry, and stir through until just well combined (do not overmix). Pour into a lightly oiled round cake pan. Bake for 26-28 minutes until golden and a toothpick inserted in the center comes out clean. Let cool.

When the cake is almost cool, place the ice cream in the refrigerator to soften. Slice the cooled cake into strips roughly 1"-1½" thick. Place the slices on the bottom of an 8"x12" (or similar) baking dish and distribute the banana slices over top. Spoon roughly ¾ of the caramel sauce over the bananas, followed by the crushed pecans. Spread the softened ice cream over top, trying not to disturb the toppings (doesn't have to be smoothed out). Place the whole pecans on top, and drizzle with the remaining caramel sauce. Cover the dish tightly with plastic wrap and place in the freezer for the ice cream to harden and the dessert to set. Before serving, remove from freezer for 5-10 minutes to let the dessert soften a little, then cut into squares.

Makes 8 or more servings.

Carob-Coconut-Pecan Cookies

Wheat-Free

When testing these cookies, many people told me that these were their favorite. This surprised me, since carob can sometimes be disappointing for those expecting chocolate. But the ingredients combine so well in this cookie that even if you love chocolate (as I do), you will love these cookies too!

1 cup	**spelt flour (see note)**
1 tsp	**baking powder**
½ tsp	**baking soda**
½ cup	**unsweetened shredded coconut**
¼ cup	**unrefined sugar**
¼ tsp	**sea salt**
⅓ cup	**pure maple syrup (a little generous)**
1 tsp	**pure vanilla extract**
½ tsp	**coconut extract**
¼ cup	**canola oil (a little generous)**
⅓ - ½ cup	**carob chips**
⅓ - ½ cup	**toasted pecans (see Cooking Notes, p. 167)**

Preheat oven to 350°F (176°C). In a bowl, sift together the flour, baking powder and baking soda. Add the coconut, sugar, and salt, and stir until well combined. In a separate bowl, combine the maple syrup with the vanilla and coconut extracts, then stir in the oil, carob chips, and toasted pecans and stir through. Add the wet mixture to the dry, and stir through until just well combined (do not overmix). Place large spoonfuls of the batter on a baking sheet lined with parchment paper, flattening them just a little. Bake for 11 minutes, until lightly golden (if you bake for much longer, they will dry out). Let cool for no more than 1 minute on the sheet (again, to prevent drying), then remove them with a large spatula and transfer to a cooling rack.

Makes 8-10 large cookies.

You can use unbleached all-purpose wheat flour in this recipe as well. Use less, though; measure out 1 cup, then remove 3 tablespoons.

Cashew-Chocolate Crumb Ice Cream Pie

I am a huge fan of ice cream cakes and pies. They can be made in advance, and are sure to please even the fussiest eaters! This one is a new favorite, with a chocolate crumb crust and rich cashew-chocolate topping.

Crust:

1¾ cup	chocolate cookie crumbs (see note)
¼ tsp	sea salt
3½ - 4 tbsp	thick honey alternative (e.g., brown rice syrup)
1 tbsp	cashew butter

Filling:

1 2-pint tub	(946-ml) soy ice cream (e.g., Soy Delicious Chocolate Velvet)

Topping:

¾ cup	non-dairy chocolate chips
¾ cup	plain non-dairy milk (reserve ½ cup)
⅓ cup	cashew butter
⅛ tsp	sea salt
1 tsp	pure vanilla extract

Preheat oven to 350°F (176°C). Prepare the crust: in a bowl, combine the cookie crumbs and salt and stir through well. Add the honey alternative and cashew butter and mix through with your fingers until crumbly and holding together somewhat when pressed. Transfer mixture to a large pie dish, pressing it into the bottom and sides of the dish. Bake for 10-12 minutes, then remove. While the pie cools, place the ice cream in the refrigerator to soften.

Use vegan chocolate cookies or animal crackers and grind in a food processor until fine and crumbly.

In a small saucepan over medium-low heat, combine the topping ingredients (except the reserved ½ cup of milk) and stir frequently until mixture is melted and well combined. Be sure not to boil; reduce heat if needed. Turn off heat, add reserved ½ cup milk, stir until smooth and let cool. Scoop the softened ice cream into the cooled pie crust, distributing as evenly as possible. Place the pie in the freezer to harden the ice cream again. Once ready, pour on the cooled topping, rotating and tipping pie to evenly cover. Return to freezer to harden, then remove to cover with plastic wrap and return to freezer until serving. To serve, let pie sit at room temperature for about 5 minutes, then slice.

Chocolate Hemp Squares

Wheat-Free
Option

These squares are incredible! A nut butter-cereal crumb base smothered in a soft chocolate coating. They store great in the freezer too, if you can get them there!

⅓ cup	hemp seed nut butter
¼ cup	almond or cashew butter
⅓ cup	pure maple syrup
¼ tsp	sea salt
1 tsp	pure vanilla extract
1 cup	cereal crumbs (see note)
¼ - ⅓ cup	vanilla other non-dairy milk
¾ cup	non-dairy chocolate chips (see note)

In a medium saucepan over medium-low heat, combine the hemp seed nut butter, almond or cashew butter, maple syrup, and sea salt and stir through until warm (don't let it boil) and well combined. Remove from heat. Add the vanilla and cereal crumbs and stir through until well incorporated, then pour the mixture evenly into a lightly oiled 8"x8" cake pan (use a small piece of parchment paper to press it down without sticking). In a bowl over simmering water (not boiling), combine the soy milk and chocolate chips and stir until melted and smooth. Let cool a little, then pour evenly over the mixture in the cake pan. Refrigerate until completely cooled, then cut into squares.

Makes 16 squares.

I use cereal crumbs as an alternative to cookie crumbs to give these cookies some texture in the nut butter layer. The cereal makes them healthier and less sweet, and you can use whatever cereal you have on hand; simply purée it in a food processor. I like to use cereals that are whole-grain but also tasty, such as Oaty Bites or Mulitgrain Oat Flakes, both produced by Nature's Path. For wheat-free squares, choose a cereal without wheat products.

A time-saving tip: instead of melting the chocolate chips with the soy milk, you can omit the milk and fold in the chips when you add the cereal. Or, after you have the mixture in the pan, press the chips into it while it's still warm.

Chocolate P-Nut Butter Squares

For those of you who adore the marriage of chocolate and peanut butter, this square is for you! A silky smooth layer of peanut butter cream covers an oat base, topped off with a silky layer of chocolate.

Oat Base:

1 cup	quick oats
½ cup	barley flour (see note)
1 tbsp	unrefined sugar
¼ tsp	sea salt
¼ tsp	baking soda
3 tbsp	pure maple syrup
2½ tbsp	canola oil

Peanut Butter Center:

½ cup	natural peanut butter
⅓ cup	unrefined sugar
½ tsp	sea salt
½ cup	plain non-dairy milk

Chocolate Topping:

¾ cup	non-dairy chocolate chips
⅓ cup	plain non-dairy milk

Preheat oven to 350°F (176°C). To prepare the oat base: in a large bowl, combine the dry ingredients, then stir in the maple syrup and canola oil. Stir through until well combined; the consistency will be crumbly yet hold together somewhat when pressed. Transfer to a lightly oiled (or lined with parchment paper) 8"x8" pan and press in evenly. Bake for 15 minutes, then remove and transfer to a cooling rack.

> You can use unbleached all-purpose flour if wheat is not a concern for you.

While cooling, prepare the peanut butter center: in a saucepan over medium heat, combine all the ingredients. Stir the mixture occasionally until it becomes smooth and uniform, and thickens (do not let it boil). It will be loose and separate initially, then will thicken to a creamy texture. At this point, pour mixture evenly over the oat base and refrigerate for 15-20 minutes.

In the meantime, prepare the chocolate topping: in a small saucepan over low-medium heat, combine the chocolate chips and milk. Stir occasionally, until the chocolate and milk melt together and are smooth with no separation of the mixture. Remove from heat. Once the oat base has chilled, pour the chocolate topping evenly over top (the chocolate topping can cool somewhat). Refrigerate again until completely cool and cut into squares.

Makes 12-16 squares.

Coconut-Lime Cookies

Wheat-Free
Option

A tangy-sweet cookie that's an exotic change from traditional cookie flavors.

¼ cup	unsweetened shredded coconut
¼ cup + 2 tbsp	unrefined sugar
1 - 1½ tsp	lime zest
¼ tsp	sea salt
1¼ cup	unbleached all-purpose flour (see note)
1 tsp	baking powder
1 tsp	baking soda
⅓ cup	pure maple syrup
2½ tbsp	freshly squeezed lime juice
1 tsp	pure vanilla extract
¼ - ½ tsp	coconut extract
¼ cup	canola oil (a little generous)

Preheat oven to 350°F (176°C). In a bowl, combine the coconut, sugar, lime zest, and salt, and sift in the flour, baking powder and baking soda. Stir until well combined. In a separate bowl, combine the maple syrup with the lime juice, vanilla, coconut extract, and canola oil, and stir until well mixed. Add the wet mixture to the dry, and gently fold and stir through until just well combined (do not overmix). Place large spoonfuls of the batter on a baking sheet lined with parchment paper, and flatten a little. Bake for 11 minutes, until lightly golden (if you bake for much longer, they will dry out). Let cool for no more than 1 minute on the sheet (again, to prevent drying), then remove them with a large spatula and transfer to a cooling rack.

Makes 10-12 medium-large cookies.

For a wheat-free version, use white spelt flour , but add an additional ⅓ cup.

Crispi Squares

Wheat-Free

A twist on the classic rice crisp square, with the addition of nuts, hemp seed nuts, cranberries, and of course, some chocolate!

½ cup	**peanut butter (or combination of peanut butter and nut butters such as almond, cashew, or hemp nut seed butter)**
½ cup	**maple syrup**
¼ tsp	**sea salt**
1 - 1½ tsp	**pure vanilla extract**
2¾ - 3 cups	**rice crisp cereal**
¾ cup	**hemp seed nuts**
¼ cup	**dried cranberries**
¼ cup	**toasted almond slices (or other nuts) (see Cooking Notes, p. 167)**
½ cup	**non-dairy chocolate chips or carob chips**

In a large pot over medium-low heat, combine the peanut butter/nut butters, maple syrup, and sea salt, and stir through until warm and melted together (don't let it boil). Stir in the vanilla extract, then stir in the remaining ingredients except the chocolate chips. Once these ingredients are well incorporated, add the chocolate chips and stir through quickly (so they don't melt too much). Quickly transfer mixture to an 8"x 8" cake pan and press in evenly (use a small piece of parchment paper to press it down without sticking). Refrigerate until completely cool, then cut into squares.

Makes 16 squares.

Delish Date Squares

Wheat-Free Option

My mother asked for a new date square recipe, so I got to work! I loved my mom's date squares growing up, and these are much like hers, but with a twist of lemon (or orange), and of course no butter. Hope you like 'em, Mom!

Filling:

2 cups	**pitted dates, roughly chopped**
½ cup	**water**
	juice from 1 lemon + water to make ½ cup (see note)
¼ tsp	**sea salt**
1 - 1½ tsp	**lemon rind (from 1 lemon) (see note)**

Crust:

2 cups	**quick oats**
1 cup	**unbleached all-purpose flour (see note)**
¼ cup	**unrefined sugar**
½ tsp	**sea salt**
½ tsp	**baking soda**
⅓ cup	**pure maple syrup**
¼ cup	**canola oil**
1 tsp	**pure vanilla extract**

Preheat oven to 350°F (176°C). For the filling: in a saucepan over medium heat, combine the dates, water, lemon juice with water, and salt. Cook for 8-10 minutes or more, until the dates break down and the mixture smooths out, stirring occasionally (reduce heat if too bubbly). Remove from heat and stir in the rind. For the crust: in a large bowl, combine all the dry ingredients. In a small bowl, combine the maple syrup, canola oil, and vanilla. Add the wet mixture to the dry, and stir through until well combined; the consistency will be crumbly yet hold together somewhat when pressed. Transfer about ⅔ of the mixture to a lightly oiled (or lined with parchment paper) 8" x 8" pan and press in evenly. Pour the date mixture on top, then sprinkle on the remaining crust mixture and press down gently. Bake for 28-32 minutes, until golden brown. Transfer to a rack to cool, then cut into squares.

Makes 16 squares.

You can substitute fresh orange juice and rind in place of the lemon. Whichever you choose, zest the fruit first and then squeeze out the juice.

For a wheat-free version of the crust, use spelt flour.

Double Chocolate Almond Explosion Cookies

Wheat-Free
Option

Critics of vegan cookies beware: this one will have you eating your words … and the cookies!

1 cup	**unbleached all-purpose flour (see note)**
¼ cup	**cocoa powder**
1 tsp	**baking powder**
½ tsp	**baking soda**
3 tbsp	**toasted almond slivers (see Cooking Notes, p. 167)**
3 tbsp	**non-dairy chocolate chips**
¼ cup	**unrefined sugar**
¼ tsp	**sea salt**
⅓ cup	**pure maple syrup (a little generous)**
1 tsp	**pure vanilla extract**
½ tsp	**almond extract (optional)**
¼ cup	**canola oil (a little generous)**
2 - 3 tbsp	**non-dairy chocolate bar, broken in small chunks, or chocolate chips (for topping)**
3 tbsp	**toasted almond slivers (for topping)**

Preheat oven to 350°F (176°C). In a bowl, sift in the flour, cocoa powder, baking powder, and baking soda. Add the almonds, chocolate chips, sugar, and salt, and stir until well combined. In a separate bowl, combine the maple syrup with the vanilla and almond extracts, then stir in the oil until well combined. Add the wet mixture to the dry, and stir through until just well combined (do not overmix). Place large spoonfuls of the batter on a baking sheet lined with parchment paper. Take 1 or 2 chocolate chunks and a pinch or two of almonds and gently press into each cookie, flattening cookies a little. Bake for 11 minutes, until just golden (if you bake for much longer, they will dry out). Let cool for no more than 1 minute on the sheet (again, to prevent drying), then remove with a large spatula and transfer to a cooling rack.

Makes 8-10 large cookies, or 12 smaller ones.

Unbleached all-purpose flour produces a more decadent cookie with classic taste and texture. You can, however, use whole-wheat pastry flour and still have a cookie that is fantastic (really!). For a wheat-free version, use spelt flour, but add another ¼ cup.

Easy Caramel Sauce

Wheat-Free

Caramel is not often found in vegan desserts, since it's traditionally made with cream and/or butter. I have a particular fondness for caramel, however, so I've created this quick, no-fuss sauce that's perfect when it's warm and drizzled over your favorite non-dairy ice cream. Also try it to top a pie, such as the Banana Hazelnut Cream Pie (p. 117), and check it out in the Caramel Pecan Ice Cream Pan Cake (p. 118).

¾ cup	vanilla non-dairy milk (can use plain)
½ cup	unrefined sugar (see note)
½ tsp	sea salt
1 tbsp	arrowroot powder (a little generous)
2 tbsp	non-dairy milk (to dissolve arrowroot)
½ tsp	pure vanilla extract
⅛ tsp	butterscotch or rum extract (optional)

In a saucepan over medium heat, combine the milk, sugar, and salt and heat for 5-7 minutes, stirring frequently, until the sugar dissolves. In a small bowl, combine the arrowroot and the 2 tbsp milk and mix until smooth. Add the arrowroot mixture to the saucepan, stirring continuously. Increase heat to medium-high, continuing to stir frequently, until the mixture comes to a boil. Let boil for a minute or so until the mixture has thickened some, then remove from heat and stir in the vanilla and butterscotch or rum extracts. Let cool before serving (the sauce will thicken more as it cools, but if you do want it even thicker, reheat it and add more arrowroot combined with milk, and bring to a boil once more).

The darker the sugar you use, the darker, more strongly flavored your sauce will be. For instance, dehydrated cane juice crystals will produce a light sauce, sucanat will produce a slightly darker sauce, and date sugar or muscovado sugar will create an even darker color with a deeper flavor. You can combine varieties if you like!

Fudgy Brownies

Wheat-Free Option

So rich and fudgy, it's hard to believe these brownies have no eggs or butter. My first cookbook, *The Everyday Vegan*, has a recipe for a brownie that's more like cake than fudge; to appease both sides of the brownie debate, I created these contenders!

¾ cup	unbleached all-purpose flour (see note)
⅓ cup	more unbleached flour or whole wheat pastry flour (see note)
⅓ cup	cocoa powder
1 tsp	baking powder
¾ cup + 1 tbsp	unrefined sugar
⅓ cup	ground chocolate chips (grind in a food processor)
½ tsp	sea salt (a little generous)
1 tbsp	arrowroot powder
¼ cup + 2 tbsp	plain soy milk or other plain non-dairy milk
3 tbsp	pure maple syrup
⅓ cup	canola oil
1 tsp	pure vanilla extract

Preheat oven to 350°F (176°C). In a bowl, sift together the flours, cocoa powder and baking powder. Add the sugar, chocolate chips, and salt, and stir until well combined. In a separate bowl, combine the arrowroot with several tablespoons of the milk, stirring through until smooth, then add the remaining milk and other wet ingredients and stir until well combined. Add the wet mixture to the dry, and stir through for about ½ minute or so. Pour evenly into a lightly oiled (or lined with parchment paper) 8" x 8" baking pan. Bake for 23-25 minutes, then remove from oven and let cool in the pan, running a spatula around the outer edge to loosen. Once cooled, cut into squares.

Makes 12-16 brownies.

For wheat-free brownies, use white spelt flour, but add an extra 2-3 tbsp (in addition to the ¾ cup + ⅓ cup).

Gingered Pear Crisp

Wheat-Free Option

A festive twist on a fruit crisp that combines sweet pears with the tang of cranberries and the mild heat of fresh ginger. While warm, serve topped with a little vanilla soy ice cream or soy yogurt for a distinctly delicious dessert.

Pear Base:

3 tbsp	pure maple syrup
1 tsp	arrowroot powder
5	fresh pears, peeled, cored and cut into thick slices or cut in chunks (roughly 4½ cups)
3 tbsp	dried cranberries
2 - 2½ tsp	freshly grated ginger
2 tsp	freshly squeezed lemon juice
⅛ - ¼ tsp	ground cardamom
⅛ tsp	sea salt
⅛ tsp	allspice

Topping:

½ cup	quick oats
¼ cup	ground oats (see Cooking Notes, p. 167)
¼ cup	unbleached all-purpose flour (see note)
¼ cup	toasted almond slivers (or other toasted nuts) (optional) (see Cooking Notes, p. 167)
¼ cup	unrefined sugar
¼ tsp	sea salt
3 tbsp	canola oil
1 tbsp	pure maple syrup

Preheat oven to 350°F (176°C). For the pear base: in a large bowl, combine the maple syrup with the arrowroot and stir until arrowroot is dissolved. Add the remaining pear base ingredients, and toss through until well combined. Transfer to a lightly oiled 8" x 8" baking dish. In another bowl, combine all the topping ingredients, and use your fingers to work the mixture until just crumbly. Sprinkle the topping over the pear mixture, distributing evenly. Bake for 30-35 minutes, until golden and a little bubbly. Serve hot or warm.

Makes 4-5 servings.

You can use whole-wheat pastry flour if you like, or for a wheat-free version, spelt flour.

Hazelnut Cardamom ("Chloe") Cookies

Wheat-Free Option

At our house, we often give our food "names" associated with family and friends for fun with our daughter Charlotte. She has Kate soup, Nanny beans, and of course, these Chloe cookies, in honor of her friend! It's a great way to encourage kids to try different foods by associating them with familiar names (even though these cookies don't require much coaxing!). These treats are great for adults too; they're fragrant with cardamon, and are not overly sweet. (If giving to little ones, pick off large pieces of hazelnuts, or crush them well.)

½ cup	unbleached all-purpose flour (see note)
1 tsp	baking powder
1 cup	ground oats (see Cooking Notes, p. 167)
¼ cup	unrefined sugar
¼ tsp	ground cardamom
¼ tsp	sea salt
¼ cup	pure maple syrup
1 tbsp	water
1 tsp	pure vanilla extract
1 tsp	hazelnut syrup
¼ cup	canola oil (a little generous)
3 - 4 tbsp	toasted hazelnuts, skins removed and lightly crushed or chopped (see Cooking Notes, p. 167)

In a bowl, sift in the flour and baking powder. Add the remaining dry ingredients and stir until well combined. In a separate bowl, combine the maple syrup, water, vanilla, hazelnut syrup, and oil, and stir through until well mixed. Add the wet ingredients to the dry, and stir through until just well combined. Place tablespoonfuls of the batter on a baking sheet lined with parchment paper. Take a little of the chopped hazelnuts and press them gently into the center of each cookie. Bake for 9-10 minutes (if you bake for much longer, they will dry out). Let cool for 1 minute or so on the sheet (again, to prevent drying), then transfer to a cooling rack.

For a wheat-free version, use spelt flour, but add an extra 2 tbsp.

Makes 18-22 cookies.

Homestyle Chocolate Chip Cookies

Wheat-Free Option

Any vegans missing that classic home-made chocolate chip cookie indulgence? Well, now you can indulge without need for the dairy, eggs, white sugar, or even refined flour if you choose. One other bonus: these are super-easy to make!

1 cup	**unbleached all-purpose flour (see note)**
1 tsp	**baking powder**
½ tsp	**baking soda**
¼ cup	**unrefined sugar**
¼ tsp	**sea salt**
⅓ cup	**pure maple syrup**
¼ tsp	**blackstrap molasses**
1 - 1½ tsp	**pure vanilla extract**
¼ cup	**canola oil (a little generous)**
⅓ cup	**non-dairy chocolate chips**

Preheat oven to 350°F (176°C). In a bowl, sift in the flour, baking powder, and baking soda. Add the sugar and salt, and stir until well combined. In a separate bowl, combine the maple syrup with the molasses and vanilla, then stir in the oil until well combined. Add the wet mixture to the dry, along with the chocolate chips, and stir through until just well combined (do not overmix). Place large spoonfuls of the batter on a baking sheet lined with parchment paper and flatten a little. Bake for 11 minutes, until just golden (if you bake for much longer, they will dry out). Let cool on the sheet for no more than 1 minute (again, to prevent drying), then transfer to a cooling rack.

Makes 8-10 large cookies.

Unbleached all-purpose flour or spelt flour produces a more classic cookie taste and texture, but you can use whole-wheat pastry flour and still get a delicious cookie. For a wheat-free version, use spelt flour, but add an extra ¼ cup.

Make a really special dessert treat: ice cream cookie sandwiches. Using two cookies that have been completely cooled in the refrigerator, spread some softened soy ice cream on the underside of one cookie, then place the other cookie on top. Wrap in plastic wrap and freeze until firm!

Kamut-Hemp Chews

These cookies have a sweet, nutty taste and a light, crunchy texture from the kamut flour. Tasty and healthy!

1 cup	kamut flour
½ cup	barley flour
1½ tsp	baking powder
¼ tsp	sea salt
⅛ tsp	cinnamon (optional)
½ cup	maple syrup
¼ cup	hemp seed nut butter (see note)
2 tbsp	almond butter (see note)
1 tsp	pure vanilla extract
½ tsp	almond or cherry extract
2½ tbsp	canola oil
3 - 4 tbsp	toasted almond slivers (see Cooking Notes, p. 167)

Preheat oven to 350°F (176°C). In a bowl, combine all the dry ingredients, sifting in the baking powder. In a separate bowl, combine the maple syrup with the nut butters, then mix in the extracts and canola oil. Add the wet ingredients to the dry, and stir through until smooth. Place tablespoonsfuls of the batter on a baking sheet lined with parchment paper (space them out as much as possible), flattening them a little. Press an almond sliver or two gently into each cookie. Bake for 11-12 minutes, until the cookies are just golden (if you bake for much longer, they will dry out). Let cool on the pan for 1 minute (again, to prevent drying), then transfer to a cooling rack.

Makes 21-24 cookies.

You can use all hemp seed nut butter or all almond butter if you like, or other combinations of the two to make the full amount (¼ cup + 2 tbsp). You can also substitute other nut butters (cashew, hazelnut) or peanut butter.

Maple Walnut Cookies

Wheat-Free Option

The flavors of the popular ice cream variety, but in a cookie! The spelt version of this cookie is also excellent. Try adding some chocolate chips too!

1¼ cup	**unbleached all-purpose flour (see note)**
2 tbsp	**unrefined sugar**
¼ tsp	**sea salt**
1½ tsp	**baking powder**
½ tsp	**baking soda**
½ cup	**pure maple syrup**
1 tsp	**pure vanilla extract**
1 tsp	**maple extract**
¼ cup	**canola oil**
½ cup	**toasted walnuts, lightly broken or crushed (reserve some for top of cookies) (see Cooking Notes, p. 167)**

Preheat oven to 350°F (176°C). In a bowl, combine the dry ingredients, sifting in the flour, baking powder, and baking soda, and stir until well combined. In a separate bowl, combine the maple syrup with the extracts and canola oil, then add the walnuts (reserving some), and stir until well mixed. Add the wet mixture to the dry, and stir through until just well combined (do not overmix). Place large spoonfuls of the batter on a baking sheet lined with parchment paper. Place reserved walnuts on top of some or all of the cookies. Bake for 11 minutes, until just golden (if you bake for much longer, they will dry out). Let cool for no more than 1 minute on the sheet (again, to prevent drying), then remove with a large spatula and transfer to a cooling rack.

Makes 9-11 large cookies.

You can use whole-wheat pastry flour instead of white flour and still have a delicious cookie. For a wheat-free version, use spelt flour, but add an extra ⅓ cup.

Peanut "Better" Cookies

These taste as good as the peanut butter cookies you enjoyed growing up – maybe "better"!

1 cup	unbleached all-purpose flour (see note)
1 tsp	baking powder
½ tsp	baking soda
2 tbsp	unrefined sugar
¼ tsp	sea salt
⅓ cup + 1-2 tbsp	natural organic peanut butter
½ cup	pure maple syrup
¼ tsp	blackstrap molasses
1 tsp	pure vanilla extract
3 tbsp	canola oil

Preheat oven to 350°F (176°C). In a bowl, sift in the flour, baking powder, and baking soda. Add the sugar and salt, and stir until well combined. In a separate bowl, combine the ⅓ cup of peanut butter with the maple syrup, molasses, and vanilla, then stir in the oil until well combined. Add the wet mixture to the dry, stir through, and as it is coming together, stir in the remaining 1-2 tbsp of peanut butter (not completely; leave bits of peanut butter throughout the batter). Place large spoonfuls of the batter on a baking sheet lined with parchment paper, and press with the tines of a fork to flatten gently and give that classic peanut butter cookie look. Bake for 11 minutes, until just golden (if you bake for much longer, they will dry out). Let cool for no more than 1 minute on the sheet (again, to prevent drying), then remove them with a large spatula and transfer to a cooling rack.

Makes 8-10 medium-large cookies.

You can use whole-wheat pastry flour instead of white flour and still have delicious cookies. For a wheat-free version, spelt flour works wonderfully (I actually think it's better than regular wheat flour), but if using, add an extra ¼ cup.

Pineapple Lemon Bars

Wheat-Free Option

A sweet and tangy cookie bar made for coconut and pineapple enthusiasts!

Bottom Layer:

1⅓ cups	ground oats (see Cooking Notes, p. 167)
⅓ cup	unsweetened shredded coconut
2 tbsp	unbleached all-purpose flour (see note)
¼ tsp	sea salt
⅓ cup	pure maple syrup
2½ - 3 tbsp	freshly squeezed lemon juice
3 tbsp	canola oil

Filling:

1 8-oz can	(228-g) crushed unsweetened pineapple (roughly 1 cup packed)
3½ - 4 tbsp	pure maple syrup
2 tsp	arrowroot powder
1½ - 2 tsp	lemon rind (from 1 lemon)
1 tsp	pure vanilla extract
few pinches	sea salt

Topping:

⅓ cup	ground oats
1 tbsp	unrefined sugar
1 - 2 tsp	canola oil
pinch	sea salt
	extra lemon rind, if any left

Preheat oven to 350°F (176°C). For the bottom layer: in a bowl, combine the ground oats, coconut, flour, and salt and mix well. Add the maple syrup, lemon juice, and canola oil and stir through until well combined. Transfer to a lightly oiled (or lined with parchment paper) 8" x 8" baking dish and press into the base of the pan (use a small piece of parchment paper to press it in without sticking). For the filling: in a saucepan over medium heat, combine the pineapple, maple syrup, arrowroot, lemon rind, vanilla, and salt and bring to a boil until it thickens, then remove from heat. Pour evenly over the bottom layer in the pan. In a small bowl, combine the topping ingredients, and work together with your fingers until crumbly. Sprinkle on the topping, and gently press it into the filling a little. Bake for 24-27 minutes, until just golden. Cool completely, then cut into squares.

For a wheat-free version, use spelt flour.

Makes 12-16 bars.

Raspberry Frosted Cake with Chocolate Cream Center

This cake takes time to prepare, but it isn't difficult at all, and the extra time is worth it. The velvety raspberry frosting pairs perfectly with the vanilla cake and chocolate cream; a wonderful cake for a birthday or other special occasion!

Cake:

2 cups	unbleached all-purpose flour
1 cup	unrefined sugar
2½ tsp	baking powder
½ tsp	baking soda
½ tsp	sea salt
1½ cups + 1 tbsp	plain non-dairy milk
½ cup	unsweetened applesauce
1½ tsp	pure vanilla extract
½ - ¾ tsp	freshly squeezed lemon juice
¼ - ⅓ cup	canola oil

Preheat oven to 350°F (176°C). In a large bowl, combine the dry ingredients, sifting in the flour, baking powder, and baking soda, and mix until well combined. In a separate bowl, combine the wet ingredients. Add the wet mixture to the dry, and stir through until just well combined (do not overmix). Pour into two lightly oiled round cake pans. Bake for 26-28 minutes until golden and a toothpick inserted in the center comes out clean. Let cool completely before frosting.

Chocolate Cream Center:

¾ cup	non-dairy chocolate chips
½ cup	plain non-dairy milk

In a bowl over a pot of simmering (not boiling) water, combine the chocolate chips and milk. Stir frequently, until the chips are melted and the mixture is smooth. Remove from heat and refrigerate to completely cool.

Raspberry Frosting:

1 300-g pkg	frozen raspberries (roughly 3 cups)
1 cup	unrefined sugar
2 tbsp	pure maple syrup
2 tbsp	canola oil
⅛ tsp	sea salt
1 tsp	lemon rind
1 12-oz pkg	(349-g) silken-firm tofu (e.g., Mori Nu brand)
1½ tsp	pure vanilla extract
2 tbsp	plain non-dairy milk
1 tbsp	agar powder

In a small saucepan over medium-low heat, heat the raspberries; keep covered but stir occasionally, until the raspberries start to liquefy. Place a fine strainer over a bowl and pour the raspberries and juice through; press them through with a spatula to extract as much juice as possible. Discard the seeds (see note). Return the raspberry juice to the saucepan over medium-low heat and add the sugar, maple syrup, canola oil, and salt. Heat until the sugar is dissolved, stirring occasionally. In a blender or food processor, purée the tofu and vanilla until very smooth; stop to scrape down the sides of the bowl as needed. In a small bowl, combine the agar with the milk. Add the agar mixture and lemon rind to the raspberry mixture, whisking continuously. Increase heat to medium-high and bring to a boil, stirring occasionally, then reduce heat to low and simmer for a few minutes until the agar is fully dissolved. Remove from heat. In the blender or food processor, while puréeing, add the raspberry mixture to the tofu and purée until smooth, scraping the bowl again as needed. Transfer the processor bowl to the refrigerator to chill (see note). Once cool, reblend the mixture before using, processing for a few minutes until very smooth again.

Spread the chocolate cream on top of the first cake layer. Place the second cake layer on top and spread on the raspberry frosting (either all over the cake, or over top to drip down the sides). Refrigerate for a couple of hours to set before slicing.

Makes 8 servings.

Instead of discarding the raspberry seeds, you can them into a jam. Mix in several tablespoons of pure maple syrup to taste, then refrigerate!

After chilling the raspberry frosting, you may think you have made a mistake because it gels and becomes thick. But don't panic! After several minutes of puréeing, the frosting will smooth out; the longer you process it, the smoother it will become. If the frosting has become too thick, and is not smoothing out after being processed for a few minutes, add a tablespoon or two of non-dairy milk and purée again. Don't add too much, though, as the cream must be thick or it won't hold on the cake.

Sublime Chocolate Bark

Wheat-Free

This chocolate bark has become a holiday tradition at our house; I make several batches using different fruits and nuts, and then place them in holiday gift bags to give out as Christmas presents. They're a huge hit, and are usually eaten up too quickly, sometimes before others can get a taste!

18 - 20 oz	**(500-575 g) semi-sweet non-dairy callebaut chocolate, broken into chunks (or roughly 3½ cups if using chips) (see note)**
¾ - 1 cup	**toasted nuts (e.g., pecans, almonds, hazelnuts), skins removed (see Cooking Notes, p. 167) (see note)**
¼ - ⅓ cup	**crystallized ginger, chopped into very small pieces (see note)**
¼ - ⅓ cup	**dried fruit (e.g., cranberries, raisins), chopped into small pieces (see note)**

In a bowl fitted over a saucepan filled with water, place most of the chocolate (reserving a few chunks). Bring the water to low-medium heat until simmering, but not boiling (reduce the heat if it begins to boil). Let the chocolate melt, stirring occasionally, taking care not to let any steam or water get into the chocolate (a must; the chocolate will seize if any water gets into it while it melts or after it has melted). Once melted, stir in the reserved chocolate chunks until they have just melted, then stir in the nuts and dried fruits. Pour immediately onto a rimmed baking sheet lined with parchment paper and refrigerate (be sure to keep it level) until completely cool and set. Once cooled, break off into pieces and store in plastic wrap in an airtight container, or package in gift bags.

You can use another dark chocolate other than callebaut in this recipe, but be sure it's a similar high quality one. You can also use a combination of semi-sweet and bittersweet chocolate, using bittersweet for roughly ¼ - ½ of the total amount.

Use toasted nuts and dried fruits in combinations and amounts that you like. You can also "top" the bark once the mixture has been poured onto the baking sheet. For instance, try an espresso-themed bark by stirring in toasted almonds and a few coffee beans, or a sprinkle of espresso chocolate chips on top. Or a PB&J theme, by stirring in some peanuts and dried cherries or raspberries, and then a sprinkle of peanut butter chips!

Feeding Your

Vegan Baby

& Toddler

Introduction

Starting your baby on solid foods is an exciting time, but it can also be a bit intimidating. For the first time, baby is consuming something other than breast milk, which is such perfect food for your little one: conveniently available, always the right temperature, and baby always enjoyed it. Now, you have to think about feeding new foods to baby, with all that entails.

When I began feeding solid foods to my daughter Charlotte, my naturopath, Dr. Trang Duong, gave me a very useful Food Introduction Schedule (p. 142)[1]. Following this chart, in combination with my consultations with Dr. Duong, gave me the reassurance I needed that I was feeding my daughter the right foods at the right times. Charlotte readily accepted most foods in each age grouping, and did not experience any food reactions or allergies or digestive difficulties.

With Dr. Duong's permission, I have revised and reproduced this chart to exclude animal products (which are crossed out in this version). It was interesting to note, however, that for people eating the standard American diet, it is recommended that animal products not be introduced to infants until at least 12 months. Even then, only goat's milk is introduced, with meat added at 18 months, and cow's milk and eggs after two years. This approach differs from how most parents feed their infants; many often introduce meats and eggs as early as six months of age.

It is important to note that regardless of how you choose to feed and introduce food to your child, babies and children should routinely be seen for well-baby/child visits with your doctor to monitor growth, weight gain and developmental milestones. While this schedule identifies age ranges for introduction of different foods, these are not set in stone. Some foods can be introduced earlier for individual children, if the child has not had any reactions and is assessed ready to move to the next stage. Dr. Duong has made modifications for some patients, and your doctor may do the same.

For more information on specific nutritional requirements for vegan babies and children, see *Becoming Vegan* by Vesanto Melina and Brenda Davis, and *New Vegetarian Baby* by Sharon Yntema and Christine Beard.

1. For resources used by Dr. Duong, see page 144.

Food Introduction Schedule

Age	Fruits	Vegetables	Grains	Protein	Oils	Other
6 - 9 mos	Blackberries Blueberries Peaches (cooked) Pears (cooked)	Artichoke Asparagus Beets Broccoli Carrots Leafy greens (collards, bok choy, swiss chard, spinach, kale, etc.) Parsnip Squash Sprouts (puréed) Sweet potato Turnip Yams Zucchini		Breastmilk		
9 - 12 mos	Apples (cooked) Apricot (cooked) Avocado (mashed) Cherry (pitted and mashed) Grapes (cut/raisins Kiwi Nectarines Papaya Pineapple Plum/Prunes	Brussel sprouts Cauliflower Celery Cucumber Green beans Green peas Green/red peppers Onion/garlic String beans White potato	Amaranth Buckwheat Millet Quinoa Rice Wild rice	Breastmilk	Canola Flax Olive	

12 - 18 mos	Figs Mango *Orange/Citrus Raspberry Raw apples/apricot/peach *Strawberry	Cabbage *Corn Eggplant Kelp/Spirulina *Tomatoes	Barley Kamut Oats Rye Spelt	Breastmilk Beans and lentils Seeds and seed butters (hemp, pumpkin, sesame, sunflower) Soy products/milk ~~Goat milk & yogurt~~	Hemp Pumpkin Sesame Sunflower	Blackstrap molasses (small quantities)
18 - 24 mos			**Wheat	Breastmilk *Nuts and nut butters (almonds, cashews, walnuts, pecans, etc.) ~~Animal flesh (fish, chicken, pork, beef)~~	Nut oils (ex: walnut, almond)	
2-3 yrs				**Peanuts and peanut butter **~~Cow milk~~ **~~Eggs, Shellfish~~		

* moderate to high potential for allergic reaction, delay introduction as late as possible

** high potential for allergic reaction, delay introduction as late as possible

Notes: Introduce foods one at a time, and after nursing. Add only one new food every 3 days, and watch for signs of allergies between each food introduced (see list of allergy symptoms below). Don't be discouraged if a child rejects a food at first. Reintroduce foods in a few days to a couple of months. Baby may surprise you with a new love for the "new" food! For infants with a history of strong allergic reactions, apply new food to the cheek first and wait 20 minutes to see if cheek reddens. If cheek is not red, apply food to infant's lips; if still no reaction, give ½ teaspoon or less of the food and observe over 4 hours for reactions. If no allergy symptoms, then give 1 teaspoon of food and increase serving by 1 teaspoon every 4 hours.

Symptoms of Allergy

Rash around mouth or anus	Eczema or cradle cap	Behavioral changes	Skin reactions
Redness of the cheeks	Diarrhea or mucus stools	Insomnia	Dyslexia
Black circles under eyes	Constipation	Food rejection	Colic
Runny nose	Hyperactivity or lethargy	Asthma	Gas/Bloating
Recurrent colds	Irritability	Severe seasonal allergies	

Food Introduction Schedule reprinted with permission of Trang Duong, Registered Midwife, Naturopathic Physician.

Infant Digestion and the Food Introduction Schedule

At first glance, the Food Introduction Schedule seems restrictive, since it recommends that many foods that parents typically feed their infants in the early months be delayed until they are at least twelve months of age. Once you study the schedule a little closer, however, and then begin the program, you will realize it is not complicated at all, and you will soon see the value of delaying certain foods. I followed this schedule fairly closely after my daughter turned six months old. She did not have any digestive troubles or allergic reactions to the new foods; she didn't experience any gas, bloating, constipation, diarrhea, or rashes, and she readily accepted and enjoyed most of the foods in each age grouping.

Unfortunately, most people assume it's normal for babies to have digestive difficulties. In fact, because our children's digestive systems develop rapidly in their first few years, many discomforts and troubles can be avoided simply by delaying the introduction of certain foods. An infant's digestive system is too immature to digest most solid foods. The digestive lining (wall of the intestinal tract) is highly permeable to large molecules of food in the early months of life. Most food sensitization occurs during baby's first year; gradual maturation occurs over their first three to four years, which is why children under the age of five are particularly vulnerable to food allergies.

The enzymes required for protein digestion are already well developed in the newborn at term. For carbohydrates, a process of adaptation is required for babies to digest starches. Undigested starches may interfere with the absorption of other nutrients and result in a failure to thrive. The enzyme needed to begin starch breakdown in the mouth (saliva) is not present in sufficient amounts until five to six months of age, and the enzyme required for starch digestion in the small intestine is not present until nine months. This enzyme does not reach fully mature levels until about eighteen months, which correlates to the presence of molar teeth. The lactase enzyme required for milk sugar digestion is present at birth and rises rapidly in response to lactose in breast milk. For fat digestion, enzymes are present at levels of 50 percent of that for adults, which is sufficient for breast milk fat digestion. In addition, human breast milk contains lipases that enhance fat digestion and absorption by 95 percent.

Given that an infant's digestive system requires years to fully develop, it is essential that we introduce foods at the proper time. Adding certain foods too early can result in food allergies, digestive difficulties, and poor immunity. The next section offers examples and suggestions for using the foods in each stage of the Food Introduction Schedule. These ideas will make preparing foods for your baby and toddler easy and fun!

References:

Akre, James, ed. *Infant Feeding: The Physiological Basis*. Bulletin of the World Health Organization, Supplement to Vol. 67, 1989. P. 56-57.

Joneja, Janice, Ph.D., RDN. *Food Allergies & Intolerances*. Second Edition: Vancouver: J.A. Hall Publications, 1988. P. 28, 251-263.

Kimmel, Martha and Kimmel, David. *Mommy Made and Daddy Too!* Revised Edition. New York: Bantam Books, 2000.

Lair, Cynthia. *Feeding the Whole Family*. Revised Edition. Seattle: Moon Smiles Press, 1997.

Yaron, Ruth. *Super Baby Food*. Second Edition, Revised. Archbald, PA: F.J. Roberts Publishing Co.

Breastfeeding

Breast milk is the best food for your baby. According to the Canadian Paediatric Society and the Dietitians of Canada, infants should be breastfed exclusively until the middle of the first year, and continue to be breastfed after the introduction of solid food up to two years of age or longer. Continued breastfeeding is recommended to 2 years of age or longer.[2]

The World Health Organization agrees, identifying research that shows that exclusive breastfeeding for the first six months is the optimal way of feeding infants. Thereafter, infants should receive complementary foods with continued breastfeeding up to two years of age or beyond.[3]

Exclusive breastfeeding until the middle of baby's first year is the best means of preventing allergies, in addition to the mother's avoidance of the most allergenic foods during the last trimester of pregnancy and during lactation.

Vegans should be aware that babies need DHA in their diet for their first two years. DHA is a long-chain fatty acid important for brain development and vision; it must be obtained through the diet during an infant's early years. It is found naturally in mammalian milk, but not in soy milk, soy formula, or any other plant-based milks. Therefore, if you will not or cannot breast feed during your child's first two years, I suggest that you speak with a trusted, knowledgeable naturopath or physician for more information about DHA to determine what options will work best for you and your growing baby.

For more information about the importance of breastfeeding, see *Dr. Jack Newman's Guide To Breastfeeding*.

2. Canadian Paediatric Society: *www.caringforkids.cps.ca/babies/Breastfeeding.htm*
3. World Health Organization: *www.who.int/child-adolescent-health/nutrition/infant_exclusive.htm*

Foods For Each Stage

What follows is a breakdown of each stage of the Food Introduction Schedule, offering you different food preparation and cooking ideas, tried and tested, as your infant grows older. These are examples of what foods I fed my own daughter through the various stages of her early life, and how I prepared them.

From birth to six months, babies should be breastfed exclusively, as previously indicated. In some situations, your baby may be able to start solids earlier, at around five months, but be sure to discuss this with your physician or naturopath in more detail before doing so.

During baby's early months, introduce foods gradually and in small amounts. Refer to the notes on the Food Introduction Schedule (p. 142) for more information about testing foods and identifying possible allergic reactions.

These examples do not use measured ingredients or amounts; parents of new and growing babies are busy enough that they don't want to have to measure out ingredients, or follow precise recipe instructions for food that baby may not even like! Instead, each section gives you general directions, examples, and ideas to help you feed your children healthy, tasty food.

A selection of fruits and veggies can be introduced at this age. Try to choose organic foods, fresh or frozen depending on availability.

Blackberries/Blueberries

Fresh berries: Purée until smooth.

Frozen berries: Thaw a little; purée until smooth. Warm up by placing in a bowl or cup on a larger bowl of warm water (i.e., a warm water bath).

Cooked Peaches/Pears

Peel and remove seeds/pits. Cut into chunks. Steam until soft. Cool and purée until smooth.

Asparagus/Broccoli/Carrots/Parsnip/Turnip/Zucchini

Peel vegetables where necessary. Cut into chunks. Steam until soft. Cool and purée until smooth; use a little water or breast milk to thin out if needed.

Asparagus and zucchini steam the quickest, followed by broccoli. Carrots, parsnips, and turnips take the longest.

Leafy Greens
(Collards/Bok Choy/Swiss Chard/Spinach/Kale)

Cut or tear greens into pieces. Steam until just tender. Cool and purée until smooth; use a little water or breast milk to thin out if needed.

If using spinach, try to buy organic. It can be one of the produce items most heavily treated with pesticides.

Yams/Squash

Bake whole at 400°F (204°C) for 40 minutes or more (see paragraph below) until soft when pierced. Once cool to the touch, scoop out flesh. Cool and purée or mash; use a little water or breast milk to thin out if needed.

The baking time will depend on the size of your yam or squash. This method of cooking is easier than steaming, which would involve peeling and chopping these vegetables, which are very hard when raw. Plus, they taste better when baked.

This stage really opens up a world of new foods for your baby. Some wonderful grains can be introduced, as well as beans and lentils, and several oils.

Apples

Peel and core. Cut into chunks. Steam until soft. Cool and mash or purée until smooth.

You can also use an organic unsweetened applesauce.

Apricots/Nectarines

Peel and remove pits. Cut into small pieces, or mash or purée until smooth.

Avocadoes

Cut in half and remove peel and pit. Mash or purée until smooth, or cut into small pieces.

Avocadoes were a big hit with my daughter at this age, and they still are. They provide healthy fats and can be easily mixed with other vegetables and grains at this stage and onwards.

Bananas/Kiwi/Papaya

Peel; remove seeds from the papaya. Cut into small pieces, or mash or purée until smooth.

Grapes/Cherries/Plums

Remove seeds/pits. Cut into small pieces.

Use organic cherries and grapes (and raisins), since conventionally grown varieties rank as among the highest for pesticide residues.

Pineapple

Remove peel and tough inner core. Cut into very small pieces or purée until smooth.

Feed only small quantities of pineapple to your baby. Too much can make his/her mouth sore.

Raisins/Dried Apricots/Prunes

Combine with a little water, breast milk, or rice milk and purée until smooth. Alternatively, reconstitute in boiled water to soften and chop a little.

Cauliflower/Celery

Cut into chunks. Steam until soft. Cool and purée until smooth; use a little water or breast milk to thin out if needed.

cont'd

Cucumber

Peel if desired. Remove seeds. Purée until smooth or cut into very small pieces.

Green Peas

Soak frozen peas in a small bowl of boiled water for 5 minutes or until warm. Purée or mash until smooth.

Green Beans/String Beans

Trim ends off and remove strings along the seams. Steam until soft. Cool and purée until smooth, or chop finely.

Green and Red Bell Peppers

Remove cores and seeds and cut into chunks. Steam until soft. Cool and purée or mash until smooth, or chop finely.

Bell peppers are typically heavily treated with pesticides, so try to use organic if you can.

Potatoes (white)

Bake whole (do not wrap in aluminum foil) then peel, or remove peels and boil. Cut into small pieces or mash with a little water, breast milk, or rice milk, and some oil such as olive or flax.

Potatoes are another vegetable that typically have a lot of pesticide residues. Opt for organic if you can.

Non-Gluten Grains (Amaranth/Buckwheat/Millet/Quinoa/Rice/Wild Rice)

Refer to the Guide to Cooking Grains (p. 164) to prepare these grains.

- Cool and combine with mashed avocado, oils, and/or veggies.
- Purée a little to soften if baby does not like whole grain texture (e.g., rice).
- Combine looser grains like quinoa with mashed potato or avocado to thicken the mixture to spoon-feed your baby.
- Combine stickier grains like amaranth or short-grain brown rice with looser vegetable purées like beans or bell peppers, or with a fruit for a baby cereal.
- Combine cooked grains, such as quinoa with brown rice, or millet with wild rice, and purée with rice milk and/or oils if desired.

Shorter grains of rice (arborio, short-grain brown rice) are the stickiest, while longer grains (basmati, wild rice) are drier and more separate. Some of these grains may be new to you too, so you may wish to prepare small amounts first to see if you and your baby will like them.

cont'd

When you find grains that baby really likes, cook in large batches and freeze in small separate portions. When ready to use, thaw in the refrigerator, or soak in boiling water (as with frozen green peas) and then drain. Some grains will be a little watery when thawed, but will take on a good texture when mixed with other foods like avocado. Freezing makes food preparation much simpler.

In addition to whole grains, don't hesitate to give your baby some foods made from refined flours. This applies now and later as you introduce gluten grains and wheat. For instance, in the 12-18 months stage, you can give your toddler some white spelt bread rather than whole-grain spelt bread. Whole grains offer more nutritional value, but small amounts of refined breads, cereals, and pastas are fine. Vegan babies will consume a lot of fiber, particularly in these early months, and some refined products help limit some of this fiber intake while adding necessary calories.

Examples of convenience foods made from these grains that can be used at this stage include:

Rice Cereal: Look for organic rice-based cereals, such as from Healthy Times. Frozen organic raspberries and blueberries are good to mix with these cereals. Let the berries thaw a little in some boiled water. Drain and then mix in with the cereal along with some fortified rice milk.

Rice Pasta: Cook rice-based pasta well so that it is quite soft. Mix with mashed avocado or other mashed veggies or oils. Puréed soups can also be used as sauces to toss into pasta. I used my "Puréed Curried Squash and Yam Soup" from page 85 of my first book *The Everyday Vegan*. You can use this recipe or a similar puréed vegetable-based soup.

Rice Breads: Try to find some rice-based breads. They are sometimes dry, and you may want to moisten them a little with oil or rice milk and cut into small pieces. You can also make breadcrumbs from rice breads to add to veggie purées and age-appropriate soups.

Rice Cheeses: Your child might enjoy some rice cheeses. VeganRella is one option; it can be cut into small pieces or melted a little to soften (be sure to cool, though).

Rice Milks: While rice milks cannot substitute for breast milk and cannot be used for formula, small amounts can be used at this age to moisten cereals, bean mixtures, grains, etc, and in recipes like rice puddings and baked goods. Look for fortified rice milks with natural ingredients and higher fat content.

Rice Crackers: Rice crackers make good teething biscuits. Some brands are softer than others. Keep in mind that they are low in fat and do not have a lot of nutritional value, so make sure baby doesn't fill up on them.

cont'd

Buckwheat Pasta: Noodles made from buckwheat are often called soba, which are long like spaghetti. They can be found in most grocery stores, sometimes in the Asian foods section. Check the ingredients list to confirm that they only contain buckwheat, since some brands combine buckwheat with other ingredients. The texture of soba noodles is quite nice; cook until soft, then chop and feed to baby as is or mixed with veggies, avocado, etc.

Other non-gluten grain-based cereals and crackers: Look in the health food section of your grocery store for cereals and crackers that are rice-based or even made from ingredients such as amaranth. These may be great snack and finger foods.

Lentils and Beans

Refer to the Guide to Cooking Beans (p. 165) to prepare different varieties of beans.

- If using canned beans, try to buy organic, and be sure to rinse thoroughly before using.
- Mash with oils, avocado, grains, and/or cooked veggies and spoon-feed to baby.
- Squish whole beans a little and let baby work at eating them with his/her fingers.
- Add beans to pastas and soups, and purée a little for baby if needed.
- Purée into a paste with olive, hemp, or other oils and feed straight from a spoon.

Start with softer varieties of beans that are easiest to digest. These include lentils, adzuki, black-eyed peas, and split peas. Lentils are a wonderful choice because they don't require soaking and they cook quickly; they also have a very soft texture and mild flavor for baby. Red lentils cook the fastest, and are also the mildest tasting among lentil varieties. Harder beans are, not surprisingly, more difficult to digest. Examples include chickpeas (garbanzo beans) and kidney beans.

As with grains, you can cook large batches of beans and then freeze in small portions (refer to the Guide To Cooking Beans, p. 165). As a side note, beans freeze much better than grains. Their texture does not change much, so you can use them frozen in almost all recipes that require them (unlike frozen grains, which I only use in soups or baby food because they become too watery). When ready to use, thaw frozen beans in the refrigerator or soak in boiling water for a few minutes, then drain.

You can also buy convenience foods made with organic beans, including:

Pea and Bean Soups: Try a few varieties of canned organic vegan soups. You will find several options including split pea, white bean, and lentil. Some are thick and hearty, and you can stir in some oils to give baby healthy fats. For some of the thinner soups, add some dense grain like millet or rice bread crumbs to help thicken. In the 12-18 month stage when your baby can eat more grains, you can add bread or cracker crumbs made from spelt, kamut, or rye. Check the ingredients on these soups to choose varieties that don't have more allergenic ingredients like tomatoes.

cont'd

Bean Spreads: You can buy prepared bean spreads to mix with some veggies or grains. It's tricky at this stage, though, because some dips may be spicy or have seeds or nuts in them, so check for these and other ingredients. By making your own, you can control the spices and add healthier fats. Make a large batch and freeze small portions. In later months, seeds can be included, at which time you can make or buy hummus. Most kids love hummus, as long as it doesn't have too much garlic. My recipe for Creamy Hummus (p. 62) is very mild in garlic and delicious. You can make it at this stage for baby without the tahini and lemon juice, plus more olive oil.

Bean Pastas: There are some pastas made from bean flours, and I've tried one made from lentil flour (Papadini by Adrienne's Gourmet Foods). Although grainier than other pastas, they offer a great source of protein and iron, and are wheat- and gluten-free.

Oils (Olive/Canola/Flax)

- Add oils to puréed foods, as well as beans, grains, veggies, pastas, and soups.
- Toss pieces of bread or toast in oils to coat and soften them.
- Add a little oil to baby's water or milk if he/she will take it this way.

Introduce oils into baby's diet by adding a little olive, flax, and canola oil to baby's food. As you incorporate other oils (later in 12-18 months and 18-24 months), continue to include a variety of oils in your toddler's diet. It's easy to rely on olive oil alone; you probably use it a lot yourself and it tastes wonderful. But it's important to get and keep your baby's palate used to a variety of oils because each offers different nutritional benefits.

Flax oil may be a little bitter-tasting, so you might want to mix it with other oils like olive or sunflower. Another option is a product by Omega Nutrition called Essential Balance Jr., a combination of flax, pumpkin, and olive oils with a natural butterscotch flavor. It's a nice oil to use in sweeter foods like fruits, fruit purées, smoothies, puddings, soy yogurts, and warm cereals.

At this stage, several new food groups are introduced, including gluten grains, soy products, seeds, and more fruits and vegetables.

Apples/Apricots/Peaches (raw)

Core apples, and remove pits from peaches and apricots, and chop. Purée until smooth, or cut into small pieces.

If you are puréeing, peels can be left on the apples, but if cutting into pieces, you may want to remove some or all of the peel if your child finds it difficult to swallow. Smaller pieces will help them swallow the peel.

Apples and peaches are typically heavily treated with pesticides, so choose organic if you can.

Citrus

Remove peel, pith, and seeds. Cut into small pieces. Use a juicer to make fresh orange juice and try a little on your toddler.

Keep in mind that there is allergenic potential with citrus. Try in small quantities to test. Choose organic oranges and other citrus if possible.

Figs

While you may not go so far as to buy fresh figs, most people enjoy fig newtons. Wheat-free fig newtons are available; look for them at your grocery or health food stores. They make a great snack when on the go.

Mangoes

Cut along each side of the flat, oval-shaped pit. Score (cut criss-cross) flesh and press in on the skin side to turn halves inside-out and expose mango flesh to cut. Also pare the flesh remaining around the pit. Cut into smaller pieces if needed. Mash and add to warm cereals or other foods, blend into smoothies or desserts, or let baby eat small pieces with his/her fingers.

Strawberries/Raspberries

Slice or chop strawberries. Raspberries are very soft so do not need to be chopped, but you can mash them a little if you like.

When in season, these fruits are wonderful treats. Opt for organic strawberries and raspberries, since conventionally grown berries rank high for pesticide residues.

cont'd

Corn

Frozen corn kernels: Soak in boiling water until just warm. Drain and serve whole, or purée to mix with other foods.

Fresh ears of corn: Remove husks and silk. Cut into thirds or quarters. Lightly steam and cool. Drizzle with a little olive oil. Let toddler eat with hands and chew off kernels.

Corn kernels also make a great snack to bring in little containers when you go out. Corn is more allergenic than other vegetables, so introduce gradually and test on your child.

Eggplant

Remove peel and cut into chunks. Steam or bake until soft. Cool and cut in small pieces.

If baking, you can toss with some olive oil. Eggplant will soak up a great deal of oil, so it's an easy way to include extra oil in your toddler's diet plus the eggplant will be tastier. At this stage, you can give baby much of the food you eat, so you can likely give him/her dishes you are eating that contain eggplant (e.g., ratatouille, eggplant dip).

Tomatoes

Cut raw tomatoes into small pieces and mix into grains, beans, or other foods. Alternatively, try products made with tomatoes, such as pasta sauce, to mix with pastas, grains, and beans.

Your toddler may not like raw tomatoes, but will likely enjoy tomato products like pasta sauce. At this stage, many of the foods you enjoy with tomatoes and tomato products (e.g., spaghetti, lasagna, soups, casseroles) can be given to your child, with a few possible modifications (such as reducing spices). That being said, I know some toddlers who love salsa, so a little spice may go a long way with your little one!

Tomatoes are also more allergenic than other vegetables, so introduce them gradually and test on your child.

Gluten Grains
(Barley/Kamut/Oats/Rye/Spelt)

Refer to the Guide to Cooking Grains (p. 164) to prepare these grains.

- Cool and combine with beans, veggies, sauces, oils, avocado, etc.
- Use in soups, casseroles, and warm cereals.
- Chewier whole grains like kamut and spelt are good additions to soups and stews, or puréed a little for easier chewing.
- Combine with some non-gluten grains, such as rice or millet. Your toddler is already familiar with these, so mixing some in is a good way to introduce them to gluten grains.
- Oats can be used to make a hearty cereal, and if you are a little more adventurous, look for

cont'd

spelt, kamut, and barley flakes to make a warm cereal much like oatmeal.

- Barley is a hearty grain that combines well with other grains and vegetables because of its sticky texture. For a sweeter version, mix with applesauce or mashed mango. Barley is also a great addition to soups and stews because it helps thicken them.
- Make your own baked goods with ground oats, barley flour, spelt flour, and kamut flour. Look for some wheat-free recipes in this book, including Apple Oat Pancakes (p. 18), Orange-Poppy Seed Muffins (p. 39), and Banana Oat Bundles (p. 32).

When processed, many cereals, pastas, and breads are made with these gluten grains. Examples of some prepared foods include:

Spelt and kamut pastas: Cook as directed, and toss with sauce, beans, oils, veggies, etc. Your whole family can enjoy these pastas, just as you enjoy wheat- or vegetable-based pastas.

Spelt tortillas: Spread tortillas with a little bean purée, jam, mashed avocado, or melt on a little non-dairy rice cheese. Cut into squares or roll up and cut into slices.

Spelt, oat, rye, and kamut breads: You may have to visit a bakery to purchase these breads, although many supermarkets are now carrying wheat-free breads. Check the ingredients to ensure they are free of eggs and dairy. Use to make sandwiches, toast, etc. Also purée a few slices in your food processor to make breadcrumbs, and keep on hand in the freezer; you can use them to thicken soups and stews for your toddler.

Breakfast cereals: Many breakfast cereals are made from these gluten grains; check the ingredients for varieties that are wheat-free and vegan. Nature's Path has a great line of organic cold cereals, with several wheat-free varieties like Oaty Bites, Mesa Sunrise, and Millet Rice Flakes.

Frozen waffles: Look for wheat-free waffles in the health food section of your grocery store. Toast as usual, and top with a little Cinnamon Sweet Hemp Spread (p. 21) and some jam or applesauce.

Cereal bars and other snacks: Your health food store or grocery store will likely carry wheat-free cereal bars. These make a great snack when you are running out the door. Also look for crackers and biscuits; for example, both Healthy Times and Earth's Best make wheat-free teething biscuits.

Soy Products

- Cut cooked tofu and tempeh into small pieces. Let your toddler work at picking up it up with his/her hands and fingers. Pieces of tofu and tempeh are great to pack in small containers for outings and snacks. Your baby may like a little seasoning in the tofu or tempeh, but nothing too spicy. Try some of the pre-seasoned varieties that you can simply bake to save yourself time of seasoning yourself.

cont'd

- Prepare soy-based meat substitutes (e.g., soy hot dogs, veggie burgers), as directed. Cut into small pieces to avoid choking.
- Soy yogurts and puddings make a quick snack and are easy to pack for outings.
- Soy cheeses can be used to melt on bread and used in recipes. Check the ingredients to ensure they are vegan and avoid hydrogenated oils.
- Soy milks can be introduced in sippy cups to your toddler. They can also be used in cereals, puddings, and other recipes.

When choosing soy milks and other soy products, choose fortified and regular fat (rather than low-fat) options where possible. Also, remember that soy milk is not to be used as a substitute for breast milk at this age and does not contain DHA. (See p. 145 for information on breast milk and DHA.)

Soy products add versatility and are great protein sources for your toddler, but be careful not to rely too much on them. It's easy for vegetarians and vegans to consume soy milks, yogurts, puddings, tofu, tempeh, and soy cheeses to excess. Look for nut- and grain-based alternatives such as almond milk and rice cheese so that soy isn't always the only option. Also, since soy can be consumed in so many ways these days, there is no need to buy cereals, breads, and pastas with soy products in them. Look to these products to incorporate different grains like kamut, millet, and spelt that may otherwise be lacking in your diet.

Be sure to check the ingredient lists to ensure that typically allergenic foods, such as nuts and peanuts, are not included. Always choose soy products that are certified organic and do not contain genetically modified ingredients.

Seeds and Seed Butters (Pumpkin/Sunflower/Sesame/Hemp/Flax)

- Offer whole sunflower seeds and lightly crushed or broken pumpkin seeds to your toddler so they can work at picking them up with their fingers. Your little one will gradually be able to chew whole pumpkin seeds, but break them up at this stage to be safe.
- Stir sesame seeds and hemp seed nuts into your toddler's cereal, pasta, soy yogurts, etc.
- Grind seeds in a food processor until just crumbly; this will make it easy to add seeds to food. Once ground, stir into sauces, pasta, bean mixtures, mashed avocado, and warm cereal, and sprinkle on veggies, soups, and casseroles. This is a great option if your child doesn't like whole seeds.
- Sprinkle flax seeds or flax meal on food or into cereals, sauces, and fruit purées. Flax meal can also be blended into drinks and used in baking recipes.
- Pâtés made from seeds may be an option. They can be mashed and spread on bread for sandwiches. Such pâtés are usually combined with ingredients like potatoes and seasonings. Be sure that the ingredients are vegan.

cont'd

- Spread seed butters on bread or tortillas with jam. Most seed butters are not sweet, and some can be bitter, so start with a small amount for your toddler and combine with a little jam, maple syrup, or applesauce
- Stir seed butters into warm foods such as oatmeal and pasta. The butters will soften and melt into the foods giving it a slightly thicker texture. You can then add other sauces and/or oils as you like.
- Try the recipe for Cinnamon Sweet Hemp Spread (p. 21); children will enjoy the slightly sweet taste, and you will like it because it is so nutritious. You can also incorporate seeds and seed butters into many recipes including baked goods, dips, and sauces, such as Sesame Mustard Tahini Sauce (p. 56). This can be used as a pasta sauce or simply drizzled over whatever foods they are eating.

Seeds are a handy snack to take on outings. You can pack some in small containers for snacks, and mix with other foods like raisins or cranberries. There are some seasoned varieties of pumpkin and sunflower seeds available that your child might like. Avoid spicy varieties; instead, try the lightly seasoned or lightly sweetened ones.

The sticky consistency of seed butters will be a new experience for your child, and they may not be fond of it initially. Start with small amounts, about a teaspoon, just to get your child used to the new taste and texture. If they seem to dislike the stickiness, adding small amounts to warm foods is a great way to incorporate them in your child's diet. Your child will gradually get accustomed to the taste and texture of these butters, but this may not be until you start using nut butters at 18-24 months. For now, this is a great way to get these nutritious seed butters into their diets.

Seed Oils
(Hemp/Pumpkin/Sesame/Sunflower)

Use seed oils in many of the same ways you use olive, canola, and flax oil:

- Add oils to puréed foods, into beans, grains, veggies, pastas, and soups.
- Toss pieces of bread or toast in oils to coat and soften them.
- Add a little oil to baby's water or milk if he/she will take it this way.

Hemp seed oil offers a good balance of omega-6 to omega-3 fatty acids, and is not bitter-tasting. Rather, it has a nutty taste, similar to sunflower seeds. Mix it into your baby's food straight or in combination with other oils. As with flax oil, hemp seed oil cannot be heated or used in cooking. For more information on hemp seed oil, refer to the Hemp Foods section (p. 169).

As mentioned earlier, once you have introduced a variety of oils, continue to do so. Our children enjoy the foods they know, so get them used to a number of oils because they offer different nutritional benefits.

Nuts and Nut Butters

- Crush or chop softer nuts (e.g., pecans, cashews), for your toddler to eat on their own. Be sure to feed them only small pieces to avoid choking.
- Harder nuts like almonds, hazelnuts, and green pistachios should be chopped very finely or ground in a food processor and then added to your toddler's food. These nuts are really difficult to bite and chew and can be a big choking risk.
- Stir ground nuts into your toddler's cereal, pasta, or soy yogurts, or sprinkle over their meals.
- Nut butters are sweeter than seed butters so may be enjoyed more by your little one. Their sweetness also lends itself better to mixing into warm cereals, and spreading on waffles, pancakes, and breads. They can also be spread on apple slices and other fruits, and used in baking. There are a variety of wonderful nut butters available, including almond, cashew, hazelnut, and macadamia.
- Nut milks can also be introduced at this stage, and are delicious. Add to cereal, use in recipes, and try small amounts in your child's sippy cup. Almond milk is available in most health food stores; look for fortified and regular fat (not low-fat) varieties. As with the other plant-based milks, remember that they cannot be used as a substitute for breast milk.

Wheat

- Bake or sauté lightly seasoned varieties of seitan (wheat gluten). Cut into small pieces for your toddler. Leftovers make a handy item to pack for meals out of the house for your little one.
- Wheat breads, pastas, cereals, crackers, and biscuits can all be fed to your toddler.

Wheat is another food product that has allergenic risk. You may have already inadvertently introduced it in small quantities to your child, because it is used in many processed foods. Monitor your child to ensure he/she doesn't have a bad reaction to wheat or wheat products.

Keep in mind that it's still important to vary the grains in your child's diet, as well as your own. It's very easy to eat only wheat-based breads, pastas, crackers, and cereals because they are widely available and generally less expensive. However, there is much to be gained in nutrition, taste, and texture of foods by eating different grains, so try to incorporate other flours like barley and spelt, and use products made from other grains when you can. There are a number of wheat-free recipes in this book for you to experiment with.

Nut Oils (Walnut/Almond)

As with the other oils that you are using in your toddler's diet, you can now offer oils from nuts. Use these oils as you have the others, to stir into foods, drizzle over meals, or add to smoothies and drinks.

Peanuts

- Chop peanuts and let your toddler eat on his/her own.
- Grind peanuts in a food processor or chop finely and sprinkle on your toddler's food or stir into sauces, yogurts, etc.
- Spread peanut butter on bread, tortillas, waffles, pancakes, muffins, cookies, crackers, apple slices, etc.
- Mix peanut butter with mashed banana or other puréed fruit (applesauce, mashed mango, puréed strawberries) to eat with a spoon or dollop on waffles, on top of puddings, etc.
- Mix peanut butter with other nut and seed butters. For example, make pb&j sandwiches with half peanut butter and half hemp seed nut butter.
- Use peanut butter in sauces and dips (e.g., peanut sauce). While some of these sauces might be spicy, you can adjust the seasonings, and your toddler might surprise you by liking them! Your little one can dip veggies, breads, pastas in the sauce or dip, or you can use to top beans, whole grains, and other dishes.

At this age, your toddler is eating just about everything you and your family are eating; peanuts are the only vegan food item that have been delayed to this point. As most of us know, peanuts, peanut butter, and other peanut products are highly allergenic, so introduce in a small quantity to test your child. Choose organic peanuts and peanut butters when possible, and be sure to check peanut butter labels to ensure they don't contain hydrogenated oils.

Additional Notes for Feeding Baby

Organic Foods

Organic foods can be more expensive and difficult to obtain, but I believe they're worth the extra cost and effort, particularly during our children's early months and years when they go through the biggest growth and development of their lives.

There are times when organic produce is no more expensive than conventionally grown produce, and times when it can even be cheaper. Shop and compare, and take advantage of seasonal and local items where possible. Certain produce items are known to be the most heavily treated for pesticides and herbicides. For instance, strawberries, raspberries, grapes, cherries, and peaches are usually heavily treated. To keep up to date on produce items that are high in pesticide residues from year to year, visit *www.foodnews.org*.

In addition to organic produce, look for organic prepared foods like pasta, bread, crackers, cereals, baby foods, and waffles, and items like organic nut butters, peanut butter, and jams. In addition to being organic (completely or partially), these will have more natural ingredients. For example, most cereals in the regular aisles of grocery stores will have a mix of artificial colorings, hydrogenated oils, refined sugars, refined flours, and/or chemicals! The organic cereals that you find (most likely in the natural foods section of your grocery store) typically use natural sweeteners, whole grains, and are often vegan.

It is funny that health food sections of grocery stores are often called "natural foods," implying that the foods in the other aisles are "un-natural." But then, when one compares ingredient lists, it's not as inaccurate as you would think!

Prepackaged Food vs. Home-Made

The quality and freshness that comes from preparing your own baby food makes it obviously superior to prepackaged foods. It also allows you to offer a greater variety of veggies, fruit, and grains to your child. Take advantage of seasonal and local produce and prepare food items from fresh products that are appropriate for your baby's age.

Many of the commercially prepared baby foods combine ingredients such as grains and beans with veggies that may not be appropriate for the age of your baby based on the Food Introduction Schedule (see p. 142). Preparing your own ensures that you are introducing foods to your little one at appropriate times, and allows you to control the type and quality of the ingredients.

There are times, however, that you will want to rely on prepackaged baby food, and there are some good organic varieties available now. I've used two brands, Earth's Best and Healthy Times (both these companies have other baby food products including cereals and teething biscuits).

It does require more time and effort to prepare your own. However, there are techniques and ideas that can make it worthwhile.

Food Preparation Tips

To make food preparation easier, invest in one or more small food processors. The one I use simply attaches to a handblender, and is great for puréeing small amounts of food. This is important because puréeing is required during the early months of introducing solids to baby, and you may be working with many small batches of fruits or veggies. It will also work well later for puréeing seeds and nuts, not to mention your own food preparation needs, like mincing garlic. A standard blender can also be used, but you may not find it as handy for smaller batches of purées, or as easy to clean.

Since you will need to steam a lot of foods during the early months of introducing solids, some type of steaming gadget is useful. Use a steamer pot (usually purchased as part of a cookware set), a small steaming basket, or electrical steamer. Steam vegetables and fruit (where required, see Food Introduction Schedule, p. 142) until soft. Keep in mind that more nutrients are retained in fruits and vegetables if the skin is left on. Strain any stringy food items, such as green beans or celery, after blending. To loosen any thick food purées, add breast milk, boiled water, or non-dairy milk (where age-appropriate).

Prepare larger quantities than just what is needed for one meal. Purchase small, airtight containers to refrigerate or freeze small batches for later meals. Store in the refrigerator for up to 3 days or in the freezer for up to 2 months.

Rather than use a microwave to warm refrigerated or frozen food, place in a small glass or glass bowl, and submerge in a larger bowl of very hot or boiled water. It won't take more than a few minutes to warm up food that has been refrigerated – just stir through a few times. For frozen portions, you may want to add boiled water, reheat in a saucepan, or place in a heat-proof container over simmering water. Be sure to stir the food well, and test the temperature before serving.

Prepare Yourself

Likes and Dislikes: Don't be surprised if your child loves yams one week and then refuses to eat them a few weeks later; babies and toddlers can be fussy when it comes to their food. This can be frustrating when you are preparing your own. Try to go with the flow and experiment with other foods. And keep in mind, the reverse is also true: a food that your child doesn't like today might be a favorite for them a month later. Give your child many chances to get to know and (hopefully) like a new food.

Don't Force the Issue, or the Food (My Beet Story!): When my daughter was just over six months, I baked and puréed organic beets for her. She turned away, winced, and pushed out the food on her tongue, giving me every sign that she didn't want them. I stubbornly persisted and eventually managed to get several spoonfuls into her. Shortly after, as we were driving to a scheduled well-baby check-up, I was feeling mighty proud of my new food introduction success. But that all came to a halt, when she brought up all of the beet purée over herself and her car seat. In three years, that incident remains the only time she has rejected a food in such a manner, and it taught me a valuable lesson: never force a particular food on a baby. I do continue to offer certain foods that were previously rejected. Children sometimes need to have a food reintroduced several times before it appeals to them because their tastes change over time. At an early age, however, don't force the issue!

Some Food Must Be Discarded: It is part of life with a baby and toddler that sometimes significant portions of food will unfortunately go wasted. Some foods can be refrigerated and reheated later. At times, though, kids will get their hands or saliva in the food, at which point keeping it for later use is not an option for food safety reasons. As well, certain foods, such as bananas and avocados, simply won't keep once peeled and chopped. Simply use your good judgment to determine whether particular leftovers are something you would want your child to eat again.

Cooking
Guides

& Notes

Guide To Cooking Grains

Grain (1 cup dry)	Water Needed	Cooking Time
Amaranth	2½ - 3 cups	20-25 min
Barley, Pearl	3 cups	40-50 min
Barley, Whole (Hulled)	3 cups	60-75 min
Buckwheat	2 cups	15-20 min
Kamut Berries	3 cups	70-90 min
*Millet	2½ - 3 cups	18-25 min
Oats	2 - 2½ cups	15-25 min
**Quinoa	2 cups	12-15 min
Rice, Brown Basmati	2 cups	35-45 min
Rice, Brown Short-Grain	2 cups	40-50 min
Rice, Brown Long-Grain	2 cups	40-50 min
Rye Berries	3 - 3½ cups	60 min
Spelt Berries	3 cups	55-70 min
Wheat Berries	3 cups	55-70 min
Wild Rice	3 cups	45-60 min

*With millet, more water (3 cups+) and longer cooking time (25 minutes+) will yield a softer, creamier texture. For a fluffier texture like rice, less water and shorter cooking time is needed, and do not stir millet while simmering.

**Rinse quinoa before using to remove its natural bitter coating. Some brands are pre-rinsed, but some bitterness may still remain. To be sure, rinse for several minutes in a fine strainer.

Cooking Tips

For all grains, rinse before using (amaranth will need to be rinsed in a cheesecloth and quinoa in a very fine strainer). You simply need to combine the grain and cooking water, bring to a boil, then cover and reduce heat to low. Simmer for the cooking time listed above, until just before the water is completely absorbed (avoid peeking throughout the cooking, check about 5-6 minutes before you think they will be done), remove from heat and let stand for 4-5 minutes. Cooking times are a guide, and times can vary slightly.

Some grains have a nuttier flavor (e.g., quinoa, amaranth, millet) and are more separate and less sticky (e.g., millet, amaranth) if toasted before cooking. To toast, simply add to a dry skillet over medium heat for a few minutes, until there is a nutty aroma. You can also sauté with a little olive oil before adding the water. In general, if you shorten the cooking time, grains will be firmer and chewier, and if you increase the cooking time (plus a little more water), grains will be softer.

Guide To Cooking Beans

Bean	Cooking Time
Adzuki Beans	45 min - 1 hr
Black Beans	1 - 1½ hrs
Black-Eyed Peas	45 min - 1 hr
Cannellini	1 - 1½ hrs
Chickpeas (Garbanzos)	1½ - 2 hrs
Kidney Beans	1½ - 2 hrs
*Lentils, brown	30 - 40 mins
*Lentils, red	15 - 25 mins
Navy Beans	1½ - 2 hrs

*Lentils do not need to be soaked at all. Just rinse and cook.

Soaking Beans: Two Ways

First, rinse dry beans and remove any little stones or beans that are split or shriveled. Beans (with the exception of lentils) need to be soaked before cooking. This shortens the cooking time, and more importantly, helps improve their digestibility. I have never been one to soak beans overnight, but it is an easy method; simply add 3 to 4 parts water to 1 part beans and soak for at least six hours.

Another method, which I prefer, is a quick-soak through boiling. I find it very convenient, and the beans are easy to digest. Combine the rinsed beans with at least 3 to 4 times as much water in a large pot. Bring to a boil, and let boil for roughly 5-7 minutes. Turn off the heat, cover, and let sit for 1 - 1½ hours. Drain beans and rinse through again. Also rinse out your cooking pot and wipe clean with a paper towel to remove cooking residues.

Another note about digestibility: in general, beans that are classified as softer are easier to digest than those classified as hard. Examples of softer beans include lentils, adzukis, and black-eyed peas; those that are a little harder include cannellini, kidney, and chickpeas (garbanzo beans). Soybeans are the hardest bean to digest, so you may want to opt for soy products like tempeh and tofu.

Cooking Tips

To cook, combine soaked beans (either overnight or through boiling method) with 3 to 4 times as much water. Bring to a boil, reduce heat to low and let simmer partially covered until tender, using the chart above to reference average cooking times. Times will vary based on the type of bean, how long they have been soaked, and how old they are. In general, 1 cup of dried beans will yield 2 - 2½ cups of cooked beans.

Freezing

Cook your beans in large enough batches that you can freeze them. Beans freeze wonderfully, and when you need them, they will be cooked and at your fingertips. I usually freeze in 2- or 3-cup amounts, since these approximate the amounts needed for most recipes. I use small zip-lock plastic bags, or plastic containers with a firm lid; be sure that they are airtight, and that you have several of them to hold 2- to 3-cup amounts. Label to identify the type of bean and quantity.

If you want to use frozen beans right away, hold the bag or container under hot running water for a few seconds to loosen, or remove the frozen beans from their container, place in a bowl, and cover with some boiled water. Once thawed, drain and they are ready to use. You can also add frozen beans directly to soups and stews and let them thaw and cook in the dish.

Of course, canned beans can be used in a pinch as well, but your own cooked beans (particularly organic) are always the best. If using canned, always rinse and drain before using.

Cooking Notes

There are a few tips that are worth mentioning because they are used frequently in these recipes:

Ground Oats

Many of my baked goods and desserts call for "ground oats." Ground oats can be made from quick oats, which are available in grocery stores. Use your food processor and process the quick oats for a minute or so. The consistency should be similar to a coarse flour.

Roasted Peppers

You can purchase roasted red peppers in jars, or buy them in bulk at most delicatessens. This is very convenient, and it's handy to keep a few jars of roasted peppers in your pantry for quick dishes. You may want to roast them yourself, however, because they're fresher, and often taste better. Roasting peppers is not difficult, and can be done days in advance of preparing a dish.

To roast peppers, first clean and core them. Cut into quarters, lengthwise (or other large pieces). Remove any remaining seeds and white membranes on the underside of the pepper flesh. Line a baking sheet with parchment paper. Place the pepper pieces skin side up, and rub with olive oil. Preheat the oven to broil, and roast the peppers for 13-15 minutes or longer, until the skins are blistering and blackened. Remove and immediately place in bowl and cover tightly with plastic wrap. Let sit for 20 minutes or more to sweat and cool. Once cool, remove the skins. Refrigerate until ready to use.

Toasted Nuts and Seeds

Toasting nuts and seeds enhances their flavors, and recipes that use toasted nuts will naturally have deeper, richer flavors. The process is simple; it just requires an attentive eye. If you have a toaster oven, you can use it for small batches. Use your oven for larger quantities (although you rarely need more than what you can fit on a toaster oven tray).

Preheat oven or toaster oven to 400°F (204°C). Line your toaster oven tray or baking sheet with parchment paper. Bake for 7-12 minutes, or until golden and giving off a roasted aroma. Watch them carefully, as toasting times vary for different nuts and seeds, and they can turn from nicely toasted to burnt very quickly.

For recipes using hazelnuts, you will want to remove the skins. After toasting, immediately transfer hazelnuts to a bowl and cover tightly with plastic wrap. Let hazelnuts steam and cool for 5-10 minutes. Transfer to a clean towel and rub to remove skins. Some skins will be tough to remove, but that's okay, you can leave some on.

Hemp Foods

Hemp Foods

Hemp foods are not well known to most people, but are an important part of a vegan diet. They include shelled hemp seed nuts, nut butter made from these seeds, hemp protein powder, hemp flour, and hemp oil.

My recipes feature mostly hemp seed nuts, hemp seed nut butter, and hemp oil, because these are the most widely available hemp products on the market today. Hemp seed oil provides essential fatty acids, and hemp seed nuts and nut butter provide a source of complete protein in addition to the fatty acids.

Hemp Seed Oil

Hemp seed oil is nature's richest source of essential fatty acids (76 percent). It offers a good balance of Omega-6 to Omega-3 fatty acids (3.75 to 1), suitable for life-long consumption. Hemp seed oil has a light green color and a mild nutty flavor, a tasteful complement to a variety of foods. Look for hemp seed oil that is cold-pressed, unrefined, packaged without additives or preservatives, and grown without herbicides or pesticides from non-GMO hemp seed.

In addition to the recipes in this book, you can add hemp seed oil to juices, smoothies, soups, and sauces to create a rich creamy texture. It's also an excellent base for any salad dressing. You can substitute hemp seed oil for other oils in recipes that are not heated above 350°F (176°C).

Hemp Seed Nuts

Hemp seed nuts are an excellent source of essential fatty acids, which they deliver in a balanced ratio of 3.75 to 1. These nuts contain the rare fatty acid Gamma-Linolenic Acid (GLA), and are also a great source of complete protein, containing all the essential amino acids. Look for hemp seed nuts that have been packaged without additives or preservatives and grown without herbicides or pesticides from non-GMO hemp seed.

Hemp seed nuts have a pleasant, nutty flavor similar to sunflower seeds. Try them in the recipes here, and as well as sprinkled on granola and salads, added to sauces, and as a recipe substitute for some nuts and seeds. You can also enjoy hemp seed nuts as a healthy snack straight from the bag!

Hemp Seed Nut Butter

Hemp seed nut butter is one of nature's richest sources of complete protein (35 percent), and Omega-6 and Omega-3 essential fatty acids (35 percent). Look for hemp seed nut butter made from 100 percent shelled hemp seed, packaged without additives or preservatives, and grown without herbicides or pesticides from non-GMO hemp seed.

In addition to recipes in this book that feature hemp seed nut butter, use it as a spread for breads, bagels, crackers, and croissants, or combined with herbs and spices for pâtés and dips. It's also a delicious addition to smoothies, sauces, and baking. Finally, try substituting hemp seed nut butter either wholly or partially for other nut butters in recipes.

Hemp Protein Powder

Hemp protein powder is a whole food protein powder that is rich in complete protein, Omega-6 and Omega-3 essential fatty acids, and healthy dietary fiber. Look for hemp protein powder that is cold-milled from live viable hemp seed grown without the use of herbicides or pesticides.

Hemp protein powder has a nutty flavor and a deep green color. Use it to create delicious protein shakes, or add it to juices, smoothies, and green drinks.

Hemp Seed Flour

Hemp seed flour is gluten-free, an excellent source of dietary fiber, and one of the lowest glycemic flours. It's a good source of complete protein and the essential fatty acids. Look for hemp seed flour that has been cold mechanically processed, packaged without additives or preservatives, and grown without herbicides or pesticides from non-GMO hemp seed.

Hemp seed flour has a mild, nutty flavor and is a nutritious base for any baking recipe. It is frequently used in breads, muffins, and cookies. Hemp seed flour adds a nutty flavor to home-made pasta, pancakes, and pita bread. It also blends well with whole-wheat flour and can be combined with other flours, or used as an addition to gluten-free recipes.

I used Manitoba Harvest Hemp Foods and Oils hemp products in my recipe testing. The nutritional and product information outlined above pertain to their product line.

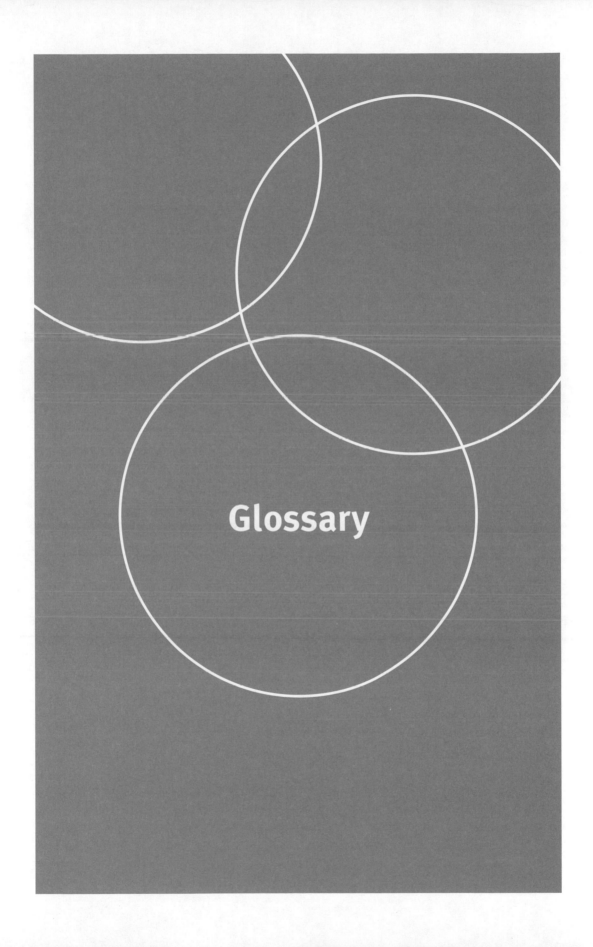

Glossary

Adzuki beans: A small, reddish bean that digests more easily than other beans and has a slight sweet flavor. Adzuki beans cook rather quickly as well (see Guide to Cooking Beans, p. 165).

Agar powder: Also called agar-agar, this powder is derived from a seaweed and is used in place of gelatin. It has no flavor, and can be easily dissolved in liquid and then gels upon cooling. Agar comes in different forms including flakes and strands. I use the powder form that is readily available in health food stores and some groceries.

Agave Nectar: Pronounced "uh-gah-vay," this is a liquid sweetener made from the juice of the agave cactus plant native to Mexico. It has a mild flavor, more neutral than honey and maple syrup. It is an excellent substitute for honey, and unlike honey, agave nectar pours and dissolves easily. It also has a low glycemic index, meaning it is absorbed slowly into the bloodstream. Available in health food stores and some groceries.

Amaranth: This very tiny ancient grain is actually a seed produced by a tall plant related to the beet and spinach family; a single plant produces thousands of seeds. Cooked amaranth has a glutinous quality, and overcooking can make it rather gummy. Try combining with other grains or use for a hot cereal for best results. Rich in protein, calcium, and iron, it is also used to make flour and in cereal and bread products.

Apple cider vinegar: This light brown vinegar is made from fermented apples, and has a mild fruity taste. Look for organic, unpasteurized apple cider vinegar that has some edible sediment floating around in strands on the bottom of the bottle (referred to as the "mother" of the vinegar).

Arrowroot powder: This tasteless thickener comes from the root of a tropical plant, and substitutes equally for cornstarch. Like cornstarch, it is dissolved in a liquid and then must be brought to a boil to reach its full thickening power. When dissolved, it is cloudy but turns clear once cooked.

Balsamic vinegar: An Italian vinegar that has become very popular for its wonderfully sweet robust flavor and relatively mild acidity.

Barley flour: Made from the barley grain, this flour works well in baking and in combination with other flours. It is light colored and mild in flavor, and can be found in health food stores and some groceries.

Barley malt: A thick, dark-colored sweetener that is used as an alternative to honey (though not as sweet) or molasses in recipes. The liquid form is used in this book and is most readily available in groceries and health food stores.

Blackstrap molasses: A syrup that is produced from the final boiling of sugar cane juice to make sugar. It is dark brown, thick, and has a strong, slightly bitter flavor. Regular molasses can be substituted and is less bitter, although it is not as nutritious. Interestingly, I use blackstrap molasses as often in soups and savory dishes as I do for baking.

Brown basmati rice: Basmati rice that is unhulled, retaining more fiber and a nuttier flavor. It does take longer to cook than white basmati rice (refer to Guide to Cooking Grains, p. 164). Basmati rice is light and dry when cooked, not sticky like other varieties. It has a long grain that gets longer when cooked, and a delicate nutty/buttery flavor (with an aroma similar to popcorn). Brown basmati rice is available in health food stores and some groceries.

Brown lentils: These are sometimes also called green lentils, and are the most common variety of lentils you see in stores. They are khaki in color, and about the size of green peas, but flattened in a disc shape. They have a pleasant earthy flavor, and cook quickly (roughly 25 minutes, sometimes longer). Like all varieties of lentils, they do not need to be soaked or precooked, as do other legumes. Before using lentils, rinse them and check to remove any small stones that may be there.

Brown rice syrup: A thick, light brown sweetener made from rice, and sometimes also contains barley malt. It is less sweet than honey or sugar, and its sugars are absorbed more slowly in the bloodstream than other sweeteners.

Cannellini beans: The Italian name for white kidney beans, these are large, white, oval-shaped beans with a smooth, creamy texture and a nutty flavor.

Capers: The unripened buds of a Mediterranean plant that are pickled in a brine to give them a salty, pungent taste. They are dark olive green and have a small roundish shape. They are widely available in grocery stores, and you will often see different sizes; the smaller ones can be more expensive and are considered better. Rinse and drain capers before using.

Cardamom (ground): A member of the ginger family, cardamom is ground from the seed that is encased in a cardamom pod. Wonderfully aromatic with a sweet flavor, this spice can be used in both sweet and savory dishes, and is a common ingredient in Indian cuisine. While the ground form is less flavorful than grinding from the seed, it is certainly an easier and more readily available form of the spice.

Carob: Available in powder and chip form, carob comes from the pod of a legume-family tree native to the Mediterranean region. It is often used as a substitute for chocolate, although it really doesn't have the same flavor. Carob is sweet in flavor where chocolate has a bitter quality. Unlike chocolate, carob does not contain caffeine. I use carob chips in this book, which are available in health food stores and some groceries.

Celery root: Also known as celeriac, this vegetable is a relative of celery that we are familiar with, but is not the root part of these celery stalks. This variety is grown specifically for its large bulbous root which, while quite unattractive, has a lovely taste with a mild celery flavor. It is similar to a turnip in shape, size and color, but is a little knobby and covered with fibrous strands and usually some dirt. It can be peeled and chopped to cook in soups and casseroles, or it can be grated or finely chopped to eat raw. When selecting celeriac, choose ones that are heavy for their size and firm, without any soft spots or bruises.

Chili sauce: A blend of seasonings that may include tomatoes, onions, chiles, garlic, vinegar, sugar, and salt. I use a very mild tomato-based sauce that adds just a little heat and some sweet and sour taste. Available in grocery stores.

Chipotle hot sauce: Chipotle chiles are actually jalapeño chiles that have been smoked and dried. They have a smoky, spicy flavor but are not as hot as some other chiles. You can find hot sauces with chipotle chiles as one of the main ingredients, and you will find that these sauces will give your dishes a little heat plus a deep, rich, smoky taste. Look for chipotle hot sauces among other hot sauces in your grocery or specialty food stores.

Coriander seeds: This spice comes from the plant of the cilantro (or coriander) leafy herb. It is common in Indian cuisine, and has a very fragrant, lemony, and slightly floral-like flavor. It can be found in grocery stores, either in the spice section or the ethnic foods section.

Curry Paste (mild): You can find small jars of curry pastes in grocery stores, usually in the ethnic foods section. These pastes range from mild to hot (I use only the mild variety in these recipes), and are a blend of different ingredients, such as coriander, turmeric, chili, onion, ginger, garlic, cumin, tomato paste, and vegetable oil. Using a good curry paste brings out a complexity of flavors in a dish that is often easier than using a variety of different dried spices and seasonings. The texture lends itself nicely to certain recipes as well. Patak's is a popular brand, and I have also used and like Minara's.

Fennel: If you like the flavor of licorice, as I do, you will love fennel. Eaten raw, its licorice or anise flavor is very pronounced and mellows if you sauté, grill, or cook it in some other way. It looks somewhat like celery, with light green stalks, but it has a whitish bulbous base, and there are some fennel ferns within the stalks. To use fennel, trim the stalks to where they meet the bulb (you can keep the leafy portion and use in stocks or as a herb). Wash and trim the bulb, cut in half and remove the core, then slice or chop as you like. When shopping, look for firm, compact clean bulbs without any blemishes and stalks that are fresh, green, and firm.

Fennel seeds: This spice adds a sweet, licorice flavor to dishes, and is often found in Italian cuisine. You can find fennel seeds in grocery stores, either in the spice section or the ethnic foods section.

Flax meal: Flax meal is made from whole flax seeds ground fine into a powdery, or mealy, form. Grinding them enhances the nutritional value of flax seeds (which are high in Omega-3 fatty acids). Flax meal also makes a wonderful egg substitute, since it becomes quite gelatinous when combined with a little water or other liquid. You can grind your own flax seeds, or buy flax meal at your local health food store or grocery store. Flax meal has a high oil content, so it can go rancid quickly; when buying it, be sure it is either refrigerated or frozen (not at room temperature), and store it at home in an airtight container in the freezer to retain its nutritional value and fresh flavor. Fresh flax meal has a pleasant, sweet, nutty flavor and aroma, whereas old or rancid flax meal will have a strong oily smell.

Flax oil: Derived from flax seed, flax oil is rich in omega-3 fatty acids. It must be kept refrigerated, and cooking destroys its nutritional value, so use it cold in salad dressings, to drizzle on food, or blend into drinks. It doesn't have a long shelf life, and so check the labels when shopping and be sure to buy it refrigerated.

Hazelnut syrup: This is a syrup used primarily to flavor specialty coffees and other drinks, and hazelnut is just one flavor among a variety you can find. I use it in desserts much like vanilla extract, to impart a lovely hazelnut flavor. Look for these syrups in specialty stores and coffee shops.

Hemp protein powder: This green protein powder is made from cold-milling the hemp seed nuts. It has a nutty flavor, and can be used in smoothies and shakes as you would other protein powders. Look for it in your health food stores. Refer to the Hemp Foods section (p. 169) for nutritional and other information.

Hemp seed nut butter: This is a nut butter made from puréeing the shelled hemp seed nut. It can be used much like other nut butters, as a spread or used in recipes. It has a greenish color and tastes somewhat like sunflower seeds. It can be found in health food stores and some groceries. Refer to the Hemp Foods section (p. 169) for nutritional and other information.

Hemp seed nuts: The hard outer shell of the hemp seed is removed to reveal the highly nutritious inner nut. Similar to sesame seeds in size with a light yellow-green color, they have a light, soft texture with a little crunch. They can be sprinkled onto salads, sandwiches, or cereals, or used in baking and other recipes. Find them in health food stores and some groceries. Refer to the Hemp Foods section (p. 169) for nutritional and other information.

Hemp seed oil: Cold-pressing the hemp seed nut produces the hemp seed oil. It has a green color and a mild nutty taste. It works wonderfully in salad dressings, and drizzled on meals, but like flax oil should not be used for cooking. It can be found in health food stores and some groceries. Buy it refrigerated and keep it refrigerated. Refer to the Hemp Products section (p. 169) for nutritional and other information.

Hoisin sauce: A thick, dark, flavorful sauce often used in Chinese cooking. It is a little spicy and sweet, made from such ingredients as soybeans, garlic, chiles, sugar, vinegar, and other seasonings. It is available in small jars in grocery stores, usually in the ethnic foods section.

Jicama: A tan-colored tuber that is shaped similar to a turnip, roundish but a little squat. It has a pleasant, crunchy texture that is similar to water chestnuts with a flavor somewhat like very mild green peas. When I have included jicama as part of a vegetable platter, it is often mistaken for apples, though it is much less sweet and doesn't discolor as apples do. When selecting jicama, look for one that is firm with unwrinkled skin and no blemishes.

Kalamata olives: This is a very popular purple-black Greek olive. They are salty and very flavorful (far more than black olives), and widely available. They can be found in grocery stores, often in the deli section (in bulk) as well as bottled in brine or vinegar among the pickles. I usually buy them pitted from the deli, since removing the pits yourself can be time-consuming.

Kamut grain (whole): Originating from Egypt, kamut is an ancient grain that is related to wheat, but can be tolerated by many with wheat allergies. The whole kernels, sometimes called kamut berries, are beige and resemble large grains of rice. Kamut is a good substitute for wheat, and has a pleasant, sweet, buttery flavor. It has up to 20-40 percent more protein than wheat, up to 65 percent more amino acids, contains more fatty acids, and is richer in magnesium, zinc, and vitamin E. The kernels take a little longer to cook than other grains (refer to Guide to Cooking Grains, p. 164), much like whole spelt and wheat berries. They have a chewy texture when cooked, so are often better mixed with other grains, or added to soups and casseroles.

Kamut flour: Made from the kamut grain, this flour can be used in breads, muffins, snack loaves, and cookies. It has a nutty flavor, but is also more coarse than wheat flour (similar texture to cornmeal flour). While this texture does not work in all baked goods, it is lovely in many, and the flour can be combined with others (e.g., spelt, oat, barley, wheat) for great results.

Maple syrup (pure): A natural sweetener from the sap of sugar maples. I use pure maple syrup in many desserts and baked goods. It's not to be mistaken for the cheaper "maple flavored" syrup that is sold for pancake topping. Pure maple syrup is 100 percent maple syrup, with no artificial flavors, colors, or additives. It is available in grocery stores, and organic varieties are available in health food stores (and some groceries).

Milk (non-dairy): There are many choices for non-dairy milks, including soy, rice, almond, oat, multi-grain varieties, and more recently, potato-based milks. Soy and rice are the most popular, and often the least expensive. Look for fortified varieties, and if using soy milk, be sure to buy those using non-GMO soybeans. There are also refrigerated milks and those packaged in aseptic containers for longer shelf life. Experiment with different milks to find ones you like, depending on what you use it for; for example, some varieties I enjoy drinking, but find their color too dark for certain dessert recipes. I keep a few types of fortified rice and soy milks on hand, as the aseptic packaging allows you to keep your pantry well-stocked.

Millet: A small, round, yellowish ancient grain that looks much like couscous. It is a good source of phosphorus, B vitamins, iron, and the essential amino acid lysine. It is easy to digest, cooks quickly (refer to Guide To Cooking Grains, p. 164), and can be used in a variety of recipes. It can be found in health food stores and some groceries.

Miso: A salty, thick paste made from fermented soybeans. Available in lighter and darker varieties, and also in combination with other grains like barley and brown rice. In my recipes, I use brown rice (or barley) miso, since it has a mellow, mild flavor. It's not very expensive, and can usually be found in grocery stores as well as health food stores.

Phyllo pastry: Paper-thin sheets of pastry, also called filo or fillo dough. Phyllo is Greek for "leaf," and this pastry is used in the popular Greek dishes spanokopita and baklava. These thin sheets look fragile, and while they can easily tear, they are also very forgiving. Most varieties are made from wheat flour, but you can find spelt versions (Fillo Factory makes one). Usually found in the freezer section of grocery stores. Check ingredients to ensure there are no hydrogenated oils or animal products.

Pine nuts: The seeds from the cones of several varieties of pine trees. They are ivory color, and while they can range shape and size, they are usually the size of orange seeds and teardrop-shaped. They have a soft texture and delicate taste, and toasting before using can enhance their flavor. Keep them refrigerated or in the freezer, since they can go rancid quickly, like many nuts. Available in grocery stores.

Pistachios: Green nuts with a delicate, slightly sweet taste and crunchy texture. Pistachios work well in sweet and savory dishes. The green/brown color is the natural color of pistachios; red pistachios have been dyed.

Portobello mushrooms: These mushrooms are known for their great flavor and "meaty" texture. They are large with a brown, round, flat cap, and a woody stem which is usually discarded or used in vegetable stocks. They are available in most grocery stores.

Quinoa: Pronounced "keen-wa," this ancient grain is small in size but big in nutrition. Quinoa is a complete source of protein, and is high in calcium, iron, and phosphorous. Uncooked quinoa resembles flattened couscous, creamy beige in color with a little ring around each grain that comes out like a tail when cooked. This ring holds the majority of quinoa's protein and gives it a very slight crunch. Quinoa cooks quickly (refer to Guide to Cooking Grains, p. 164), has a very light texture, and digests easily. It does have to be rinsed for a few minutes before cooking to remove its natural bitter coating. Look for quinoa in health food stores and some groceries.

Red lentils: These are small, pink-colored lentils that turn golden when cooked and have a mellow flavor. They cook very quickly (refer to Guide to Cooking Beans, p. 165), and like other lentils, they do not need to be soaked before cooking. They don't hold their shape at all after cooking, so they work best in soups and recipes where they will be mashed or puréed (e.g., veggie burgers, pâtés).

Red peppers (roasted): Most groceries carry jars or bottles of roasted red peppers packed in oil, vinegar, or water. You can also usually buy them bulk in the deli section of grocery stores. They are tasty and quick, and save you the time of roasting them yourself. I use Bellisima roasted red peppers packed in water with whole garlic; they have a lovely flavor.

Sesame oil (toasted): Pressed from toasted sesame seeds, this oil has a lovely deep sesame flavor and a dark golden color. Be sure to buy toasted sesame oil when recipes call for it. The lighter color sesame oil is not from toasted seeds and does not have the same intense, rich flavor. The flavor is so strong, in fact, that you need just small amounts to season dressings, sauces, and other foods. Available in grocery stores (often in the ethnic foods section) and health food stores.

Shitake mushrooms (dried): These mushrooms have a brown, sometimes flat cap with a light underside and a thin, stiff stalk. They have a great earthy flavor and a chewy, meaty texture. Dried shitakes are a handy pantry item; they have a concentrated flavor and simply need to be soaked in boiling water for 10-15 minutes to reconstitute. Dried shitakes can be purchased whole or sliced in small packages in most grocery stores (among the fresh mushrooms). They are also available in Asian specialty stores in larger volume.

Silken tofu: A smooth and silky variety of tofu sold in small, rectangular, aseptic boxes. An alternative processing of the soy milk creates a different texture than that of regular soft and firm tofu. Since silken tofu becomes so smooth and creamy when blended or puréed, it is often used to create smoothies, dips, and of course desserts. The packaging allows for a long shelf life, even without refrigerating (although I prefer to refrigerate). Mori-Nu silken tofu (soft and firm varieties) can be found in most grocery stores, health food stores, and some Asian specialty stores.

Spelt flour: Made from the whole spelt grain, this flour is available in both whole-grain and refined forms. Both substitute well for wheat flour, although you may need to adjust either reducing or increasing the amount just slightly depending on the recipe. It can be found in health food stores and some groceries.

Sugar (unrefined): Unlike commonly known white and brown sugar, unrefined sugar retains some nutrients because they are only partially refined or not refined at all. The term unrefined sugar can include such products labeled as sucanat, turbinado, and evaporated cane juice. Be sure to check the label to ensure it is unrefined; organic sugar, for example, is now popular but is not necessarily unrefined. Unrefined sugar has a golden color (light to dark beige), and some types (e.g., demerara) have granules that are a little larger than standard white sugar. Finer granules are easier to bake with; sucanat and most varieties labeled "unrefined sugar" work well.

Sunflower oil: Made from sunflower seeds, this oil is pale in color and has a very mild sunflower taste. It works nicely in salad dressings and can also be used for cooking.

Tahini: Sometimes called sesame seed butter, this paste is made from puréeing white sesame seeds. It is often used in Middle Eastern recipes such as hummus and baba ghanouj. It is found in jars among other nut and seed butters. As with all natural seed and nut butters, the oil in tahini rises to the top because there are no additives to suspend the oils, and so you simply need to stir the oil through before using and then refrigerate.

Tamari: A soy sauce made from fermented soybeans, and without the colorings and additives found in many commercial brands. Tamari is also wheat-free unlike many soy sauces.

Taro root: A high-carbohydrate tuber that is somewhat similar to potato, but a little sweeter and with some sticky consistency. They have a fibrous dark brown peel (similar to the outside of a coconut) and a white flesh speckled with some purple color. They must be cooked and can be used much like potatoes, removing the peel before or after cooking. You can find them in some groceries and Asian specialty stores. Look for ones that are firm without any soft spots or blemishes.

Vanilla extract (pure): Made from steeping pure vanilla beans in alcohol and water or in a glycerin-water base. Look for pure vanilla extract and check the labels. It's not the same as artificial or imitation vanilla extracts. These contain artificial colors and flavors, and do not have nearly the same flavor as pure vanilla. Available in grocery stores and organic varieties in health food stores.

Vegan Worcestershire sauce: A Worcestershire sauce made without anchovies. I have found two brands available in health food stores, one by Annie's Naturals and the other by The Wizard.

Vegetarian ground round (veggie ground round): A ground meat substitute made from soy protein and sometimes wheat protein (gluten), as well as seasonings. It is precooked and available in different varieties, such as regular, Italian, and Mexican. Used to replace ground meat in dishes like tacos, chili, spaghetti sauce, and shepherd's pie. Some brands are fortified with iron, zinc, B vitamins. Look for those using non-GMO soybeans. Available in health food stores and most groceries.

Wheatberries: Wheat grain in its whole-grain form, with just the inedible outer hull removed. They are brown with a roundish shape and a nutty flavor. Like whole spelt and kamut kernels, wheat berries have a chewy texture and take a relatively long time to cook (refer to Guide to Cooking Grains, p. 164). They are best combined with other grains or used in soups, stews, casseroles, or salads.

Wild rice: Not actually a grain, but a water-grown grass. Wild rice has a purple-black color, a lovely nutty taste and a chewy texture. It opens up and curls when fully cooked, exposing a white interior. Look for wild rice in health food stores and most groceries.

Index

Index

Index

Index

Index

Index

Index

Index

Dreena is a stay-at-home mother of a three-year-old and a newborn and the author of the bestselling cookbook *The Everyday Vegan*, published by Arsenal Pulp Press in 2001. She has appeared on national television and at food festivals in Canada and the United States, and has written for *Vegfamily.com* Magazine. Originally from St. John's, Newfoundland, Dreena now lives in White Rock, British Columbia.

Praise for *The Everyday Vegan*:

A flavor feast! This is a book for anyone who loves food and wants to be healthy, with great recipes that are easy and totally tasty.
  – Ingrid Newkirk, PETA

One of the most beautifully laid out cookbooks I have ever encountered. I own many vegan cookbooks, and Dreena Burton's *The Everyday Vegan* is by far one of the very best.
  – Shayla Roberts, *VegFamily Magazine*

It's the recipes that convince naysayers that vegan food can be flavorful (and full of protein). Maple Banana Loaf uses soy milk, wholewheat and kamut flours and pure maple syrup to delicious effect.
  – Jennifer Hain, *Toronto Star*

I would definitely recommend picking up a copy of *The Everyday Vegan*. Now I'm just waiting for her to come out with another book!
  – Stacey Foley, EarthSave Canada

This book is a great "all-rounder" with ideas and recipes to meet every need. Sweets lovers are especially well catered for.
  – *Veg-Feasting in the Pacific Northwest*, Vegetarians of Washington

Burton has designed these recipes for daily use; they're easy enough to put together, and there's enough variety to suit every taste.
  – Rachelle Nones, *VegNews*